Who is
NICK SAINT?

Who is NICK SAINT?

GYLES BRANDRETH

LITTLE, BROWN AND COMPANY

A *Little, Brown* Book

First published in Great Britain in 1996
by Little, Brown and Company

All characters in this publication are fictitious and any resemblance to real persons, living or dead, is purely coincidental.

A CIP catalogue record for this book
is available from the British Library.

ISBN 0 316 87979 7

Typeset in Bembo by
Palimpsest Book Production Limited,
Polmont, Stirlingshire
Printed and bound in Great Britain by
Creative Print & Design (Wales), Ebbw Vale

Little, Brown and Company (UK)
Brettenham House
Lancaster Place
London WC2E 7EN

'Know thyself?' If I knew myself, I'd run away – Goethe

Who is
NICK SAINT?

Chapter One

When I saw him that first day, standing naked in the shower, the water rippling down his chest, the soap bubbles cascading off his shoulders like champagne, I thought I had never seen anything more beautiful. Certainly I had never seen anything quite like it because, believe it or not (and I know, Misty, someone of your generation may find it hard to believe), I had not seen a man naked before. I had seen drawings and paintings and photographs (Paul gave me a copy of *The Illustrated Art of Sensual Massage* for my twentieth birthday), I had seen any number of contrived mid-shots in the movies and some ludicrous snapshots that Karen had taken of Doug the summer we went to Rhode Island, that same summer I suppose I must have seen all of Paul in bits (and at his insistence), and, of course, I saw Andrew, though only ever in the half-light when I was too shy to look and he was too shy to show. But this was different. This was an Adonis, golden, glorious, gorgeous. This was perfection.

Moments this good don't last. With his left hand my paragon of masculine magnificence turned off the shower, with his right he grabbed a towel and wrapped it around his preternaturally firm, brown stomach. Then he looked up and saw me.

'Hi.' He smiled a brilliant smile. He seemed quite unabashed. 'You're Miss Macdonald.'

'Yes, I—'

'You tried the front door, but you got no answer.'

'Yes, I—'

'So you came round the back and thought you'd take a short cut through the shower room.'

'No, I—'

He laughed. His eyes were blue, clear, cerulean. 'Hang on,' he said, disappearing into a changing booth. 'I'll make myself decent, then we'll sort you out. I don't think we were expecting you till tomorrow.'

'You weren't, but I was on standby and a seat came up so I thought I'd better take it.'

'I'm glad you did,' he said, emerging from the booth dressed in a disappointingly conventional tracksuit. 'By the way, I'm Nick Saint.' We shook hands. It was around half eleven on 9 September 1996. I'll not forget the moment.

'And I'm Kirsty Macdonald,' I said.

'I know. We all know all about you. The Head read out your CV at the last faculty meeting. Too good to be true. That was Quincy's verdict. He said you must have something to hide, some dark secret. Do you?'

We had moved out of the changing room and were climbing the three or four shallow stone steps to the archway where I had come in. 'I don't think so.' I tried to say it lightly. 'How about you?'

'Me?'

'Yes, why are you here?'

'Long story.'

'I hope you'll tell it me sometime.'

'I doubt it,' he said, not unkindly, but with an uncompromising neutrality in his tone. He wasn't passing judgment, simply relaying information.

We stepped out onto the gravel path. The autumnal sunshine was dazzling. He ran his hands through his hair, squeezing out the water. 'Let me take you to our leader. I'll show you the scenic route.'

The Thomas Browne Academy for Boys was situated at Magnolia Hall, a once-magnificent eighteenth-century Georgian-Palladian villa set on the banks of the Ashley River, thirty miles north-west of Charleston, South Carolina. The Hall, built in 1738 by the first Thomas Browne (to designs by John Webb, son-in-law of the great Inigo Jones), was the last plantation house in the area and had survived the ravages of the Union troops in the spring of 1865 only because the fourth Thomas Browne, a doctor, had persuaded his slaves to spread word that the house was being used as a smallpox hospital. The present Thomas Browne, the ninth, also styled Dr, though possibly with less justification, had managed to keep the property out of the predatory (if benign) hands of the National Trust for Historic Preservation by selling off the last of the land around the house and by opening the school as 'a foundation dedicated to educating young men of potential who do not always do well in a traditional classroom situation but who can achieve acceptable and sometimes conspicuous success when given more individualized attention'. The school – sixty students, eight nationalities, all boys, all boarders – had not itself been a conspicuous success, but for Dr Browne for nearly three decades it had been a way of life, albeit an increasingly troubled and uncomfortable one.

'That's his study,' said Nick, pointing up to a mullioned

window on the first floor. 'He sleeps there too. The rest of us are in the north wing.'

'Why are the drapes drawn?'

'Because it's not twelve yet. In the vacation, he doesn't emerge before noon. When the boys are here he's not so bad, but when it's just the two of us he lets himself go a bit.'

'Do you live here all the time?' I asked.

'Yup,' he said, and left it at that.

We came round the south-west corner of the house, past what was now the school hall (what John Webb in his original plans had described as the 'High Roome', fit to receive '*des personnes d'honneur*'), and appeared to be back where we had started.

'Isn't this where I came in?'

'It certainly is,' he said with a smile. 'Showers and changing room on the right, servants' entrance to the main house on the left. Where's your luggage?'

'I travel light.'

Nick gave me a quizzical look. 'Perhaps Quincy was right.'

'Perhaps,' I said, trying to sound mysterious, and realizing instantly that I was probably sounding embarrassingly winsome or, worse, deliberately flirtatious. 'Actually, my books and things are being sent on later. Who's Quincy?'

'One of our colleagues, Dean of Studies, no less; not that that means a lot since there are only five of us, six now with you. Quincy isn't his real name. He's just called that. They've all got funny names. It's a funny place.'

A clock began to strike the hour. 'High noon,' said Nick. 'The Head will see you now.'

Quite unselfconsciously, this walking thesaurus of all the manly virtues took my hand and led me along stone-floored passages, under stuccoed arches, through fire doors, up small sets of steps, along paneled corridors and finally up a fine oak staircase to Dr Browne's study. As he knocked on the door, Nick whispered, 'You've not met him, have you?'

'No, but we spoke on the phone. He sounded nice, but old – and quaint.'

'He's all of that,' said Nick with a smile, 'and more.'

'Come!' called a languid voice from within. Nick turned the handle and pushed open the door. Dr Browne was standing in the middle of his study, his arms outstretched in welcome. He wore a maroon velvet smoking jacket, double-breasted, with a yellow (yes, Misty, a bright, canary yellow) handkerchief protruding extravagantly from his breast pocket and a tasseled smoking cap perched on his tiny bald head which was tilted coyly to one side. He could have been posing for a picture. I supposed he was posing for me.

'My dear,' he sighed. 'You've come – on the wrong day, but to the right place and at the right time. And you are most welcome! Isn't she, Nicholas?'

'Yes, indeed, sir,' said my hero.

'And isn't she lovely?'

'She certainly is, sir.' My hero indeed!

'Now, Nicholas, be a saint. While I let Miss Macdonald into one or two of our secrets, would you search out Miss Haversham and warn her that our new colleague has arrived?'

'My dear,' said Dr Browne when Nick had left us, 'sit yourself upon the chaise longue and let me fix you a drink. An American Beauty would be appropriate, I think, don't you? A quarter of brandy, a quarter of grenadine, a quarter of orange juice, a quarter of dry vermouth and a dash of crème de menthe.'

He had bottles of all these – and many more – arranged in alphabetical order on his bookcase. As he spoke he expertly poured the ingredients into a silver shaker – rescued, he maintained, from the *Titanic* (or was it the *Marie Celeste*? – the story varied), and having shaken it with the world-weary aplomb of Carmen Miranda's leading man on the maracas, he poured the cocktail into a tall wineglass.

'I'm afraid I don't really drink,' I said.

'Quite right,' he said, downing his extraordinary concoction in a single gulp. 'Nor do I. At least, not between eight on Monday morning and four-fifteen on Friday afternoon. During those six thousand two hundred and fifty-five penitential minutes of self-imposed abstinence I spend every single moment simply thinking about what I'm going to be drinking at the weekend. For four and three-quarter days I sieve the idea of alcohol slowly through my brain. As you'll discover, I talk about drink and little else, but when the boys are around I don't touch a drop. I trust you believe me?'

'Well, yes,' I hesitated. 'Of course. Is there any reason I shouldn't?'

'None at all, except that alcoholics are notorious liars. However,' he said, draining the rest of his cocktail into the glass and adding just a dash of port – 'Cockburn's Special Reserve, ideal for everyday drinking' – 'you will find I am different. To you, Miss Macdonald, as to every one of my colleagues and to each of my boys, I tell the truth, the whole truth and nothing but the truth, so help me God. To others – the parents, the grandparents, especially the grandparents, the so-called governors, the bank, the IRS, God rot them – I tell lies. Not very good lies, not very effective lies, maddeningly lies that are never as consistent as they ought to be, but to you, my dear, I will always tell the truth.'

He downed the second drink, again in a single throw, and made a little bow. 'An Applejack Rabbit next, I think, don't you? To celebrate the new semester. Orange, lemon, grenadine and calvados. Oh, my dear, it's good to see you. Thank you for coming. Please stay. Please stay and be happy.' His face, which had been pale gray when I came into the room, was now a rosy pink, and there were tears in his eyes. 'Nicholas Saint is a good man. You'll like him. Everyone does.'

'What does he teach?'

'Everything. We all do. You'll be our only specialist. That's why I'm so delighted you're here. You'll be marvelous for morale. You'll halve the average age of the faculty at a stroke. Miss Haversham will be furious. And you'll be great for business. I won't pretend that isn't the chief reason I wanted you. Dyslexics from dysfunctional families – that's our specialty, and now we have an expert on the spot!'

'I wouldn't call myself an expert—'

'You don't have to. Leave the lying to me. Anyway, it isn't lying. It's marketing. You're an English graduate. That means you can teach English. You're a psychotherapist. That means you're a trained counselor.'

'But—'

'But me no buts, Miss Macdonald. The Thomas Browne Academy for Boys now has its very own remedial teacher and dedicated college counselor. That's what it'll say in the new prospectus. That's how it is. Cheerio!'

Dr Browne drained his tumbler of Applejack Rabbit, mopped his mouth daintily with his canary yellow handkerchief and surveyed his wall of bottles. 'Have you ever tried Turkish Blood? Half-and-half red Burgundy and Russian stout. It is quite as disgusting as it sounds.'

I got to my feet. 'I think I'd better find my room.'

'Of course. Any questions before you go? You'll be paid in cash on the last Friday in the month. Nominally, Mr Rogers is the director of finance, but in fact I handle all that side of things.'

'Is there a school timetable?'

Mr Browne laughed and put down the pewter tankard in which he had been swirling his Turkish Blood. 'Oh, yes, my dear, we're quite conventional, really. I just behave like this in the hope of seeming more interesting – to myself, if to no one else. Thomas Browne's is actually a very ordinary school run in an all too predictable way by half a dozen mainly decent, if slightly lackluster, individuals. I'm afraid our eccentricity is rather studied. When you're over fifty you'll find that struggling by on thirty thousand dollars a year is dull and dreary and a little disappointing, and if you behave like a daffy schoolmaster it makes it just a bit more bearable. Despite the impression I may have given you this morning, I am not a bad headmaster and this is not a bad school. It has become, I fear, an indifferent school. It lacks ambition, but it serves a purpose, and we have standards, of a sort. All but one of the staff are graduates and, to my knowledge, none of them has ever interfered with any of the boys. We may be unique among the boarding schools of North America! At the same time, as people, *qua* people, we're failures and we know it.'

'Does that include Mr Saint?'

'Oh no, my dear, he's quite different. Study him, and he will surprise you as no other human being has ever surprised you. Nick Saint is perfect.'

Dr Browne was right. Nick Saint was perfect.

He was wonderful with the boys. There were exactly sixty that semester, all teenagers except for three Saudi Arabian princelings aged nine, ten and eleven who doted on Nick, traipsing around after him like a trio of devoted puppies, forever demanding attention, tugging at his coat, asking for this and that. Ten minutes alone in their company and I'd have been reaching for the Prozac. Nick simply took the boys in his stride. He answered their ever-flowing stream of questions, not perfunctorily but with apparent interest and enthusiasm. He taught them card tricks, he played video games with them (and let himself be beaten, not too often, just enough), he was even happy for them to pile into the back of his ancient Mercedes and join him on shopping expeditions to Charleston or Summerville. He was like a caricature of a young dad in a TV commercial, handsome yet wholesome, athletic yet reliable, rugged but unthreatening, obviously (though not too obviously) a New Man. If a child fell out of a tree you knew this caring model of concinnity would be able to catch him safely and, more to the point, be there to catch him at exactly the moment required.

Nick Saint was perfect to look at, but he didn't seem particularly aware of his own appearance. He was perfect to be with because, quite extraordinarily for someone so devastatingly good looking, he was funny and quirky and interesting. Andrew was pretty, of course, and sweet, but even at seventeen I had realized he was essentially dull: someone to look at and stroke, but without hidden depths; without hidden shallows, come to that. What you saw was what you got. Nick was different. There was something mysterious about him, but it didn't seem contrived. He was complex and profound, but his manner was uncomplicated and open. He was rational, discreet, polished, even, but unlike Jane Austen's Mr Elliot, he was more than capable of bursts of feeling and the warmth of indignation or delight. He cared. He cared about the school. He cared about Dr Browne and the curious band of professional eccentrics who were our colleagues. Most of all, he cared about the boys. I am happy to report too that, right from the start, I believe he cared about me.

'I like you, Miss Macdonald,' he said that very first evening, as we sat on the wooden bench at the top of the Dutch Garden watching the sun disappear behind the cedar grove (the sixth Thomas Browne's contribution). 'I like you.' He said it as if he was saying it within quotation marks. There was self-mockery in it, but no parody. 'We are going to be the best of friends.'

It was a week before Nick kissed me, and then it was nothing more eventful than a chaste goodnight kiss in the corridor outside our rooms. The rooms were adjacent, the only two rooms on the top floor of the North Wing, immediately above the boys' dormitory and immediately below the water tanks. The doors to the two rooms faced one another inside a small alcove recessed from the corridor. Two people couldn't stand together in the alcove without touching. When we came up to bed at the same time, which almost invariably we did, Nick would always pause in the corridor to let me get into my room. He waited until I was inside before unlocking his own door and, once inside, I could hear him locking the door again from within. We shared a bathroom at the end of the corridor, but somehow Nick contrived never to be in it when I wanted to be, and the only really unmanly thing about him was the immaculate state in which he left it after he had been in there.

* * *

Misty, one of the many traits you and I share is insatiable curiosity. Whatever others might say, I believe this is healthy! It shows an enquiring mind and an enterprising spirit. If the Pilgrim Fathers hadn't been of an inquisitive and adventurous disposition, doubtless I'd have been born in Dumfries not Monterey. At least, I squared it with my conscience that it was in the proud tradition of my forebears that I twice attempted to get into Nick's room in the dead of night when I had heard him padding along the corridor and locking himself in the bathroom. My missions were unsuccessful. However urgent the call of nature, Nick always found time to lock his bedroom door behind him.

It is to my eternal shame that when eventually I saw inside his room I did so by taking advantage of his innate goodness. It was on my fourth Friday at Thomas Browne's. I remember it because it was my first payday there and because what happened that night changed my life. At around two in the morning there was a violent burst of rapping on both our doors. Virtually in unison we opened them to find a pair of Saudi Arabian princelings in pajamas, blue-lipped, teeth chattering, tearful.

'Zanu is sick.'

'I'm coming,' said Nick, pulling on his robe and following the boys down the corridor.

'I'm coming too,' I said. 'I'll get some water.'

I heard Nick and the boys clatter down the stairs as I went into the bathroom. I ran the cold water, filled a glass, dampened a facecloth, grabbed a towel and came out into the corridor again. I knew what I should have done; I knew what a decent person would have done. Instead, I ran quickly back towards our rooms. Holding the glass and the facecloth in one hand, and with the towel over my shoulder, I tried Nick's door. It opened easily. The door swung back. It was pitch dark. I fumbled for the light switch. I flicked it and blinked. In the far corner was an artificial Christmas tree covered with decorations and lights, and all over the walls, and over the ceiling, were pictures, drawings, illustrations, posters, photographs, all sizes, all styles, but just one image: Santa Claus.

'Oh, my God,' I thought. 'He's gay.'

Chapter Two

Misty, I want you to know that I had not gone to South Carolina in search of love. I had gone in search of happiness. It was a specific mission, a deliberate quest, in its way an academic exercise, though 'quite absurd, self-indulgent and naive,' according to Professor Atkins.

'You can't anatomize happiness, Kirsty, it's not some elusive butterfly you can pin down and dissect.' The great man – for to me, the Professor who for the past two years had been supervising my thesis (and much else in my life besides) was still a great man in his own wounded way – growled wheezily in a fair imitation of Orson Welles on the slide. 'Believe me, my dear girl, if the ingredients of happiness could be analyzed, the elixir would have been bottled years ago. You're wasting your time, you're debasing your training, you're looking for a way of avoiding reality. You are making a *huge* mistake.'

'It'll only be for a year or so.'

'Who knows?' He snorted and swung his chair round to face the window.

'I know,' I said. 'You think I'm wrong. I know I'm right.'

'"The pendulum of the mind oscillates between sense and nonsense, not between right and wrong."'

'I need to go away now,' I persisted, 'but I'll need to come back, too.'

He gazed out over the immaculately manicured lawn. 'Why? Why do you need to go away now? You have everything here – a beautiful home; fine parents; from what I can tell, good relationships, meaningful ones, whatever that means. You even have the prospect of a job that pays well and helps mend people's lives. What more do you want?'

'I want to be happy.'

'For Christ's sake, Kirsty, pull yourself together! You've just spent two years studying Jung and Adler and R.D. Laing, and now you're talking like Betty Boop. Look, honey, if you can't be happy in Monterey, California, you can't be happy anywhere.'

'Perhaps I can't be happy anywhere. That's what I need to find out.'

'Don't give me that bullshit, sweetheart. There is no crock of gold at the end of the rainbow, there is no holy grail. There may be varying states of contentment, there may be emotional equilibrium, there may be games we can play or techniques we can develop to bring balance to our lives, but there is no cute little box hidden under the Christmas tree that you can seek out, unwrap and, hey presto, there's happiness!'

'Isn't there?' I laughed.

'No, Kirsty, there is not, and you know it. Life is not a feel-good movie. Life is a roller-coaster. Some days you're up, some days you're down.' He swung his chair round towards me. 'If you want to know what happiness is, I'll tell you. At twenty it's sex, at fifty it's solvency, at seventy-five it's freedom from arthritis.'

'That isn't true.'

'Oh, no?'

'It's cynical.'

'It's shorthand. All I'm saying is what you know and know well. Contentment comes in different ways to different people at different times.'

'Then why is everyone I meet so discontented? There's more sex and more money and more pain-relieving drugs than there's ever been. How come there's no more happiness?'

'There's no pleasing some people!' The Professor roared with laughter and, with effort, propelled his huge frame out of the chair. 'I know what it is, Kirsty, my bodacious babe. You're about to find religion. You're going to disappear from our lives for a year or two and return reborn, one of those bright-eyed seraphic women who wander across campus in floral dresses greeting perfect strangers with a beatific smile and an all too bright "Good morning". That's if we're lucky. If it all goes wrong, we'll read about you when you're holed up with the crazy leader of a bizarre sect who can't tell the difference between arson and incest and sets fire to all his sisters!'

He gathered up his papers from the desk and came and put his great bearlike arm around me. We walked together towards the classroom door. He rumbled gently. 'I've said my piece. My conscience is clear. Go east, young woman, and, by the time you're through, whatever it is you think you're looking for I hope you'll think you've found it – though, for pity's sake, don't look too hard, don't let the search consume the seeker. Remember, "every form of addiction is bad, no matter whether the narcotic be alcohol or morphine or idealism."'

Professor Atkins was right. I had everything in Monterey. Mom and dad lived their enchanted lives up the valley in bucolic bliss and provided me with my own apartment over the stables. Andrew stood rock-like at the center of my angst-free network of buddies, all as witty and whacky as the cast of *Friends*. I had everything and was quite ashamed that I still felt I had nothing. 'As far as we can discern,' said Jung, 'the sole purpose of human existence is to kindle a light in the darkness of mere being.' I wasn't going to kindle any lights in the sun-soaked gloom of Monterey. Would I do any better at Magnolia Hall, on the banks of the Ashley River?

'Why here of all places? That's what I ask myself.' Miss Haversham played APHID across the top of my HIDDEN, secured twenty-two points and moved decisively into the lead. She moistened her lips, narrowed her eyes and gave a little moue of pleasure as she noted down the score. 'Playing Scrabble in the faculty room is all very well if you're a dowdy old spinster like me, but you've still got the bloom of youth on you.'

Miss Haversham was certainly dowdy, and she cultivated a brittle, birdlike manner, pernickity and a little precious, fussy rather than fastidious, that some – authors of murder mysteries, for example – might well characterize as spinsterly, but she didn't strike me as being particularly old. In fact she seemed to have reached the age when it is difficult to pinpoint an age. At times, when she had done her hair and the light was right and she gave one of her rare open smiles, she might have been thirty-eight. Tonight, at the end of yet another exacting week teaching too great a range of subjects to predominantly uninterested teenagers of markedly mixed abilities, she seemed a weary fifty-five.

I played CRUDELY and scored seventeen. 'I think I wanted to get away from it all,' I said.

'Well, you've certainly done that, and you've opened up the Triple Word Score for me. QUAY. Forty-eight, I think. Yes.' She began to look a year or two younger.

'And I wanted to spend some time with young people, with kids, trying to understand them, seeing what makes them tick.'

'Heavenly gods, spare us! Please!' Theo Quincy threw down his newspaper. 'Whatever it is you're here for, Miss Macdonald, it isn't to get closer to the children.'

'Yes, it is.'

'No, it is not. We've all ended up at Magnolia Hall for a reason, but none of us is here because of our single-minded devotion to the cause of education.'

'Perhaps not singleminded, perhaps not the cause of education even, but I do care about the children; I care greatly.'

'Methinks the lady doth protest too much,' chimed in Miss Haversham as she laid a magisterial PROPINQUITY (104) across my pathetic OFAL (12).

Quincy grinned and clapped his hands. 'If you're trying to tell me you've abandoned the charms of California and the sunny uplands of a promising career in psychotherapy for the dubious delights of getting closer to the hapless misfits whose absentee parents have decanted them into the empty vastness of Thomas Browne's so-called Academy for Boys, then I – I—' His oratorical flourish ran out of oomph. 'I just don't believe you.'

'It's true.'

'It can't be!' He thumped the table with his paper. Miss Haversham pursed her lips as the Scrabble tiles rattled. This was no time to disturb the field of play. She was about to achieve a famous victory.

'Careful now!' she tut-tutted as she pluralized my TRUCK (22) with her BREAST (29).

'Miss Macdonald is lying to us, Miss Haversham,' continued Quincy, 'and I think she ought to know, as fellow members of faculty, that we're too old, too tired, too talented to need to put up with it.'

I laughed, as Quincy intended I should. He was always passionate, often argumentative, but I never saw him truly angry. He modeled himself on James Baldwin. He hadn't read *Another Country*, let alone *Giovanni's Room*, but when he, Quincy, was quite young he had seen several TV interviews with Baldwin, then quite old, and had become star-struck. Like Baldwin, Quincy was black and gay, smoked incessantly and had the protuberant eyes and the restless energy that are sometimes associated with an over-active thyroid. Quincy, however, had neither Baldwin's political zeal nor, despite his best efforts, Baldwin's dazzling and apparently effortless way with words. The other key difference was that Quincy was British. Very much so.

'If I've not come here for the sake of the children,' I asked, 'what have I come for?'

'To escape, of course!' He lit up another Gitane, drew on it profoundly, and hissed at me, 'You're like the rest of us – you're running away.'

Miss Haversham used her last two letters ('AX, the old spelling, but it's allowed, of course') and began to tot up the final score. 'I enjoyed that,' she muttered complacently.

'Now what you're running away from, at your tender age, that's the interesting question.' He let the smoke filter slowly out of his mouth and rise into his nostrils again. 'What's your little secret, Miss Macdonald?'

Misty, I don't know if you've yet discovered the intoxicating sense of freedom that comes from the sudden realization that, in this life, if you don't want to, you don't need to answer the telephone, you don't need to open the mail and you most certainly don't need to respond to middle-aged men inviting you to reveal your little secret. You can set your own agenda. In truth, I liked Quincy, I liked Miss Haversham too; yes, I was naive, but instinctively I trusted them, and had I been able easily to articulate my 'little secret', to serve it up in a palatable package that made any sense to me and might have made some to them, I would have done so. I looked up at Quincy smiling down at me through the haze of cigarette smoke and thought, I don't have a secret past, but I do have a secret longing and yet, simple as it is, I don't believe I can express it to you without it sounding at best cutesy, at worst banal.

He persisted. 'Well, little Miss Mac?'

'Don't bully her, Theo.' Miss Haversham was gathering up the tiles. 'Shall we have another game?'

'I'm not bullying anybody. I'm just inviting Miss Macdonald to come clean with her colleagues, that's all. It's simply a matter of mutual trust.'

'You first, then,' I said. 'What's your secret?'

'*Moi?*' His bullfrog eyes bulged and he pouted as he exhaled the syenite-blue smoke. 'Shall I tell her, Miss H?'

Miss Haversham sighed and rattled the tiles in the homemade bag she had embroidered with her own version of a William Morris design. (There was an Arts and Crafts side to her nature that provoked profound, if irrational and unfair, irritation in others.) 'If you must.'

'I think I must.' He turned and presented himself towards me, arms slightly outstretched, palms outward. 'Miss Macdonald, what you see before you is a criminal on the run.'

I didn't react, either because I wasn't certain that I believed him or because he didn't seem to me to be a very menacing sort of villain.

'I trust you are suitably shocked?'

I hesitated. 'I'm not sure.'

'Oh, Miss H. She's going to be non-judgmental. How very modern.'

Miss Haversham closed her eyes for a moment and pursed her lips. 'Get on with it.'

'It's quite all right,' said Quincy. 'There are no children involved. That's a relief, isn't it?'

Miss Haversham flattened the bag of tiles in the box and reached under the table for the lid. 'Theo, get on with it.'

'There is sex, of course. And blackmail. And a touch of violence. But essentially it's a story of betrayal.' He positioned himself in front of the solid marble fireplace (courtesy of the second Thomas Browne) and prepared to tell his tale. 'I'll just give you the edited highlights. I was born in Guyana, in 1948, 14 March, same day as Albert Einstein – and Michael Caine. Not a lot of people know that.' I smiled obligingly. Miss Haversham rested her chin on her folded hands and closed her eyes.

'We were sent to London in 1952. My father worked at the High Commission. My mother was a housewife. We were black, but indisputably middle class. I was sent to a private school, a boarding school, not far from Warwick. I did rather well there. I ran faster than most of the other boys, and jumped further and higher. I was also sufficiently accomplished as an actor to persuade Mr Carson, the head of English, to produce *Othello* in my final year. "Most potent, grave and reverend signors, my very noble and approved good masters . . ."'

Miss Haversham opened her eyes. Quincy turned to the fireplace and extinguished his cigarette. 'Anyway, I made the grade at A level and, at eighteen, enrolled at Sandhurst as an officer cadet. I was a star attraction. In those days, high-achieving black people in white communities usually were. Two years later, even stronger, leaner, fitter, I passed out with flying colors – not quite the Sword of Honour, but almost – and, as a glossy first lieutenant, joined my regiment in Germany. That's when the trouble started. That's when I met Captain Kendal. He fell in love with me. It was as simple as that. Or, rather, it wasn't simple at all, because, as well as being my superior officer, he was recently married and his wife, Jodie, was newly pregnant. He was white, too, of course, gloriously white in that deliciously understated fair-haired English way. He was Christopher Robin, aged twenty-six – your age, Miss Macdonald.'

I didn't say anything. Quincy lit another cigarette.

'I was only twenty-one, but quite accustomed to people falling in love with me. It was happening all the time. I used to take it for granted, until about ten years ago, when, suddenly, it stopped. It was always white guys and always the same: a preadamite animal attraction made more enticing, and perhaps more acceptable, because I was an ebony black boy with the manner and – oh so important – the accent of a perfect English gentleman. The skin tone always fascinated them, the nature of the pores, the smell, the curious texture of the negro hair. Captain Kendal was no different from the rest – except in this. I loved him back.

'Our affair followed the course of almost every other affair in the history of human frailty. It lasted three months. Apparently, with married men, that's the length of the average affair. Did you know? I read it somewhere. Anyway, you won't be surprised to hear it began with a look – and ended in tears. Predictably the look led to a shared cup of coffee, which in turn led to a long drive through the German countryside, then to another, even longer, and then, of course, to yet another – with a picnic in the woods this time: we weren't afraid of clichés. And that was when we kissed. Ken said it was the first time for him. It might have been. Remember, we were officers and gentlemen, and he was white and I was black and this was a quarter of a century ago. So the kiss led to the regret, and then the disgust, and then the remorse and the firm resolve simply to be friends, friends in a way no one has ever been friends before, friends so close, so complete that we would be inside each other's heads – now, always, absolutely, forever – even if we could never touch. Then I had four nights' leave and Ken lied to Jodie about going to recce some future exercise and we booked into a traveling salesmen's hotel in Wuppertal. For forty-eight hours we made love, then we slept, then we sat up in bed eating sauerbrod and plotting Jodie's murder.

'It was just a game, of course. We didn't mean it. Ken just wanted her to disappear, to evaporate, so his conscience could be clear. Every which way we planned to do away with her there was never any pain, never any mess. It was vodka murder, clean with no aftertaste.

'After the statutory three months, Ken's enthusiasm began to wane; perhaps his lust was sated, or perhaps Jodie was more obviously pregnant and his conscience pricked him. Anyhow, it was all over as far as he was concerned. Indeed, he told me that not only was it all over, but it had never happened. He was quite emphatic about that. "It never happened." He chose to tell me this, *sotto voce*, early one Friday evening when we were standing together in the corner of the crowded mess and about to be called in for dinner. "It's over and it never happened." I was hurt, to be sure, but, stupidly, I was also taken by surprise. My throat went dry and my eyes filled with tears. Through a clenched jaw Ken barked noiselessly at me, "Pull yourself together. It never happened. *It never happened*." He had a glass in his right hand and was squeezing my upper arm with his left. His grip became harder, tighter. I heard myself sobbing and I couldn't see him for tears. Suddenly his glass crashed onto the parquet flooring and I felt his fist smash straight into my face.

'When I was summoned to appear before the commanding officer, I told the truth. I told the whole story, just as I've told it to you now. Captain Kendal, of course, denied it all. He said that it was a case of unrequited love, that I had developed a crush on him and that when he had made it clear that he couldn't and wouldn't reciprocate, I had attempted to blackmail him. As proof, he produced a series of letters, four in all, unsigned but typed on my typewriter. They appeared fully to justify his allegation. He maintained that while he was embarrassed by my obsession with him, disgusted by my perversion and angered by my pathetic attempts to hold him to some sort of ransom, he had been reluctant to report the matter to the appropriate authorities because I was only twenty-one and he didn't want to ruin my career. But when I had threatened him that night in the officers' mess, he had lost control and struck at me. He admitted it was wrong to have hit a junior officer, but he had been provoked. He had done nothing to encourage me, he was horrified by the way I had abused his friendship, and even more so that of his wife, but I had had my chance and had thrown it away and, yes, he would have to give evidence against me at the court martial, however reluctantly.'

Quincy paused and turned to look at me. 'Now, Miss Macdonald, whose version of events do you believe?'

'Yours, of course,' I said unhesitatingly. 'But who did they believe at the court martial?'

'We'll never know,' said Quincy, closing down his half-finished cigarette between his thumb and forefinger. 'The court martial didn't take place – or, if it did, I wasn't there. Perhaps in the army they can try you in your absence? I don't know. In the run-up to the trial I was confined to barracks and, except for two periods of exercise a day, kept under surveillance in a locked room in the hospital bay. One night, exactly a week before the preliminary hearing, at around four in the morning, I felt a hand on my shoulder. I woke at once, jumped off the bed, turned on the light. There was no one there, but on the floor by the door was an envelope. Inside it, £200 in used notes. I tried the door to the room. It was unlocked. Outside it was pitch dark, but I realized at once that my guard was not at his post. The camp itself wasn't particularly secure, more difficult to get into than out of. Within ten minutes I had made my escape. Within half an hour I had hitched a lift. By lunchtime I was on a flight from Frankfurt to Istanbul.'

'And the rest,' said Nick Saint, standing framed in the doorway, 'is history!' He came into the room, smiling indulgently at Quincy. Almost ritualistically, they slapped palms. 'Another bravura account of the Great Escape?'

'Indeed,' said Miss Haversham a little testily. She got to her feet and carefully placed the Scrabble box at her end of the mantelpiece. 'I enjoyed our game, Kirsty. Thank you. If you'll excuse me, I must get myself ready for Prayers.'

'Yes, yes, yes,' said Quincy, watching her go, 'even Miss Haversham has a secret. And, galling as it is to have to admit it to you, Miss Mac, it's considerably darker than mine.'

'You underestimate yourself, Theo,' said Nick, looking at his friend complacently. He really was quite extraordinarily handsome. He turned to me. 'Theo hasn't told you of his time in Turkey, or of the flight into Egypt yet, has he?'

'But he will!' said Quincy with energy. 'All my secrets are yours, Miss Macdonald, yours for the asking. There's no nook or cranny of my past that you can't explore, no aspect of my psyche that you can't delve into, no fantasy, no dream, no nightmare I don't yearn for you to interpret. My life, my mind, my very soul, to you they will be an open book. Posthumously, who knows, they may even become a book printed and bound, destined for the best-seller lists. Meanwhile, all my secrets are available to you, *gratis*, anytime, on a no-holds-barred want-to-know basis. I trust you completely.'

'Why?' I asked, amused as much as intrigued.

'Why what?'

'Why do you trust me?'

'Because of your training, of course. You're a psychotherapist. That much we do know. You glow with integrity. That's plain. To you, the secrets of the couch and the secrets of the common room are like the secrets of the confessional. You'll take them to the grave. Dr Browne must have seen that at once. You wouldn't be here otherwise. This place is a sanctuary simply because it's built on mutual trust. The six of us can say whatever we want to one another in complete freedom and absolute safety. Nick calls it the security of known relationships. I will tell you everything and anything you want to know.'

He paused. 'Inevitably, you will not find all our colleagues equally forthcoming. Mr Rogers, poor fellow, is frequently in denial. And my friend Nicholas here' – Quincy turned to Nick, cupped his hands oh-so-gently around his face and lightly drew his fingers down his cheeks as though he were caressing a gigantic fairy-tale peach '—young Nicholas likes to keep his own counsel. He has his secrets, of that you can be sure. Like the rest of us, he's here for a reason. What it is, we don't know. We surmise, but, as yet, we don't know. At least, not for sure.'

Embarrassed, Nick moved away. 'That's enough, Theo.'

'I've made him blush, Miss Mac. But he won't deny it. He may not share his secret with his friends, but he won't pretend there isn't a secret to be shared. That's because Nick Saint never lies. I have known him a long time and of one thing I am certain: in all his born days Nick has never told an untruth. He's odd that way. Unique.'

The telephone rang. Quincy went to answer it. 'Saved by the bell.'

Nick looked at me, smiled, and shook his head.

'It was Rogers,' said Quincy, gathering up his newspaper and his cigarettes. 'I'm required at Prayers. Our beloved headmaster has the Margaritas all lined up.' He tapped

Nick on the elbow with the paper and, as he left, offered a half-bow in my direction. 'Be good, you two. Thanks for your company, Miss Mac. I'm glad you've joined us. See if you can't unmask our hero here, but go gently. Whatever you do, don't fall in love with him. That way madness lies. *Ciao*.'

Chapter Three

Since it had become a school, Miss Haversham had been responsible for all the furniture and furnishings at Magnolia Hall. In *The Beauty of Life*, her hero William Morris had advised her to 'have nothing in your house that you do not know to be useful, or believe to be beautiful', which explained why the four whitewashed walls of the faculty room, high, wide and inviting as they were, remained starkly bare but for two items: to the right of the door, by the side of the lockers, the semester's timetable (the handiwork of Mr Rogers), and above the magnificent marble fireplace, disproportionate to it but so ravishing that it did not matter, a small watercolor of St George and the dragon by Edward Burne-Jones. To me, the glory of the painting (which glowed like an original) lay in its colors: the sleek blue-black of the dragon (in appearance not unlike one of the alligators from the Everglades), the shining young knight in his luminous ash-gray armor, his skin the palest burnished gold, his magenta cloak sharply delineated against a far horizon where indigo hills met an ivory sky. For Miss Haversham, so she told me (without elaboration), the picture's chief attraction lay in the idea it represented and the story it told. As well as George and the dragon, the painting contained another figure. In the middle distance, apparently tied to a stake, stood a wan-faced, doe-eyed, russet-haired pre-Raphaelite maiden patiently awaiting her salvation. Was this how Miss Haversham pictured herself? And, if it was, who would be her ideal St George? Dr Browne? Mr Rogers? Theo Quincy?

My own hero was standing with his back to me, his hands resting on the mantelpiece, his head bent forward, his eyes fixed on the empty grate.

'I'm sorry about Theo.'

'Don't be,' I said. 'I like him.'

'That's good,' he said, turning to face me. 'That's very good.' He sounded relieved. He grinned at me.

'What's Prayers?' I asked.

'I don't know,' he said. 'I've never been. I suppose it's a kind of senior faculty meeting, every Friday, just the four of them, at six.'

'Are they religious?'

'Not so you'd notice!' He laughed his easy laugh. 'I don't think much praying takes place at Prayers. I rather suspect that, come the end of the working week, our good headmaster is more interested in uncorking the mysteries of his cocktail cabinet than unraveling the eternal verities.' He clicked his tongue and clasped his fingers together. 'No, that's unfair. I don't know what they get up to.'

'Perhaps they're Freemasons. Or witches.' I wanted to provoke him into some sort of indiscretion. He smiled at me, not because he was taken by my suggestion but more, I imagine, because he was amused by my ploy.

He unclasped his fingers and stretched his arms wide. 'If you're still here, I'll tell you next year.'

'Why next year?'

'Because then I'll know. At the end of the summer

semester I shall have completed my tenth year at Magnolia Hall, and Dr Browne has been good enough to tell me that I shall then be eligible to attend Prayers!'

'Ten years is a long time in one place.'

'Don't we hope for an eternity in paradise?'

There was no shading of self-mockery in what he said. No hint of irony, either. He must have sensed what I was thinking. 'Okay, it's not paradise, but it's good all the same. I love the kids. I believe – I hope – the work's worthwhile.'

'Is it enough?'

'Ah, who knows? We're not all destined to change the world.'

'You might be.'

'Why do you say that?' He looked at me curiously, but without the flash of anger I had expected the moment I spoke. 'I doubt it. "He who would do good must do it by minute particulars."'

'Nick,' I said, boldly, absurdly, suddenly going way over the top, 'I'm going to tell you why I think you could change the world—'

He stepped towards me and very gently put the tips of his fingers to my mouth. 'Please don't.'

Misty, have you heard of Abraham Maslow? He was a psychologist, quite famous internationally a generation ago, a positively folkloric figure in the tiny world of Monterey because he had taught Professor Atkins. In his best-known work Maslow made a study of some of the towering figures of history – a varied group of remarkable individuals justly celebrated for their intellect and their humanity – names like Spinoza, Einstein, Thomas Jefferson, Abraham Lincoln, Eleanor Roosevelt

– people who had lived their lives to the full and left the world a better, and a different, place. Maslow concluded that these 'self-actualizers', as he called them, these quite special people who can find self-fulfillment and begin to realize all their positive potential, have specific, identifiable characteristics in common: they accept themselves and others for what they are; they perceive reality efficiently and are able to tolerate uncertainty; they are spontaneous in thought and behavior; they are problem-centered rather than self-centered; they have a good sense of humor; they are highly creative; they are resistant to enculturation, although not purposely unconventional; they are concerned for the welfare of humanity; they are capable of deep appreciation of the basic experiences of life; they are able to look at life from an objective viewpoint; they establish deep satisfying interpersonal relations with a few, rather than many, people.

Having observed Nick at close range for five weeks, having seen him walk and talk and teach and play, it seemed to me that he had all the characteristics that Maslow had identified and had them in fuller measure than any other person I had ever met. Of course, I did not know him that well and there was one area, at least in regard to me, where he did not fit the Maslow template. He was not spontaneous in thought and behavior. With the boys, certainly he was. To watch him alone with them out on the far field, conjuring up games to play (games that would take up the whole afternoon, games where he was the leader but they all played as one), joining them as they climbed higher and higher up the fantastic ilex tree, rolling with them as they tumbled helter-skelter down the river bank, he seemed completely spontaneous, fearless, free, childlike himself, but in no sense childish,

Peter Pan with the prowess of Tarzan and the wisdom of Solomon.

With me, he was different; always kind, invariably courteous in a rather old-fashioned, Southern way, but there was something in his manner that was calculated. I wanted him to be open and easy with me, as he was with the boys or with Theo. Instead he was watchful, wary, like a once-abused child.

With his hand at my mouth for that brief moment, I wanted to protrude my tongue through my lips and touch his fingertips. Fortunately I managed to contain this flicker of lunacy. I subdued the madness into words, but they were dangerous enough. 'How about love?'

Why did I say it? What was I hoping to achieve? What was I wanting to provoke? Did I expect him to come out on the spot, suddenly to reveal that he and Theo Quincy were lovers? No. Did I want him to renounce his gayness, sweep me into his arms and tell me that true love had passed him by until this very fall when I had come, explosively, into his all-but-empty life? More likely.

His hand fell to his side. He walked past me and stood gazing out of the window towards the Dutch Garden where an Italianate sun was setting very much in the manner of Sir Edward Burne-Jones. 'Love?' he said lightly. 'I love this place. In time you will too. I love my work. I love the kids.'

'And Theo?'

'I love him very much. Of course.' He had said what I had expected, what I had feared, really, but the words as he said them didn't sound as I had thought they would. 'We go back a long way.'

I was taken by surprise. 'Years and years?'

'Longer than that.'

I was confused. 'Really?'

'Whoa now!' he said, spinning round and laughing at me. 'That's enough interrogation for one day, Miss Macdonald. I thought you shrinks weren't supposed to ask leading questions.'

My cheeks burned. 'Depends on the school.'

'Are you making a case study of me, then?'

'No,' I said, and then I went too far. 'I'm trying not to fall in love with you.'

He laughed, not unkindly. 'That should be easy. I don't think romance is quite my style, do you? Anyway, what's wrong with friendship? I believe it's much underrated nowadays. Why don't we have a go at a supercharged friendship and see what happens?'

We did. And Theo came too. That Sunday, in brilliant sunshine and sky-high spirits, the three of us piled into the front seat of Nick's old Mercedes and, arm in arm, drove to Charleston. Even as we set off, I thought, consciously, 'This will be a day I shall never forget'. Frequently, as a girl, I would clamber into bed and whisper noiselessly to my pillow, 'I'll always remember what happened today, always, always', and now I can't recall any of it. I resent the way photographs conspire to distort what we remember. Effortlessly, vividly, we can bring back the most banal moments, routine family gatherings, mundane school events, vacations best forgotten, friends who weren't really friends at all, simply because there happens to be a snapshot in an album or in the drawer, but so many of the really precious days, the ones at the time we wanted to press like rare flowers into a Bible, they've gone, not just faded, they've vanished altogether. I have no photographs of that golden day in Charleston, but I remember it all the same, like a favorite movie.

If happiness is living fully in the here and now, Nick Saint was happy that Sunday. 'My friends,' he announced as he maneuvered the car through the picturesque colonial side-streets, 'we're going downtown. I want to take you on a guided tour to one of my special places.'

'A secret! A secret! He's going to spill a secret!' With his right hand Quincy rapped a manic tattoo on the dashboard.

'Don't get too excited, Theo. I'm only going to show you the house of my dreams.'

'Dreams, dreams, dreams . . .' Quincy became the Everly Brothers.

As we turned into what the traffic suggested was the city's main north–south thoroughfare, Nick leaned forward over the wheel and looked up at the buildings on either side of the road. 'This is Meeting Street. It's all here.'

Theo hummed on as Nick lovingly described each piece of history that we passed. A massive brick structure on one side: 'That's the Circular Congregational Church, the fourth on the site; the earlier ones were destroyed by earthquake and fire.'

'Earthquake and fire!' Theo erupted like an old-time preacher. 'Earthquake and fire!'

'Shut it, Theo! Now that—' it was a sort of Greek temple made of brick – 'that's the Hibernian Society Hall, founded in 1799 by eight Irishmen committed to good works and ecumenism. Tradition requires that the presidency of the society alternates between a Catholic and a Protestant.'

'You don't say!' squealed Theo in mock excitement.

'And there, the white building, that's the first fireproof

building in the United States, designed by Robert Mills and constructed in the year 1822.'

Theo whispered to me conspiratorially, 'The year 1822, Nick Saint's special year.'

'Why's that?' I asked.

'Yes, Nick,' Quincy leaned forward gleefully. 'Why is it your special year?'

Nick wouldn't be discomfited. 'Ignore him. Just be grateful we haven't got him on one of his depressive days.'

Quincy wouldn't give up the game. 'Go on, Miss Mac, ask him. See if you can squeeze the secret out of him.'

'I'm sure he'll tell me if he wants to.'

'Thank you,' said Nick. 'Thank you.' And a beat or two later, quite gently, he squeezed my arm. He pulled up at the lights, grateful to have something new to describe. 'This intersection is known as the Four Corners of Law because on each corner there's a building representing a different form of authority – the county courthouse there, the federal courthouse opposite, City Hall here and St Michael's church there.'

'George Washington prayed here,' said Theo with solemnity. 'And Robert E. Lee. In Charleston we've known 'em all.'

'We're almost there,' said Nick. We parked right outside a handsome red-brick mansion, three stories tall, set back from the street behind imposing wrought-iron railings. 'What do you think?'

We didn't say. We got out of the car. The black gates clanged noisily behind us as we crossed the courtyard and climbed the three front steps to the polished, porticoed white front door. Nick let us in. He had his own key. He turned it in the lock with care and precision, like a sophisticated safe-cracker who knows it's smarter to do the job with delicate skill than brute force.

We followed him in. Softly he closed the front door behind us and led the way through the lobby into the main hall. A shaft of bright light streamed in from one of the tall narrow windows. Nick stood in it, as in a spotlight. 'Well,' he repeated, 'what do you think?'

In front of us was a staircase, a spiral staircase, exquisite but assured, graceful, confident, rising up and up through the house with effortless, easy elegance. As we came close to it and looked up we realized that, although it rose through all three floors, at no point did the staircase touch the walls. It was simply there, floating nonchalantly in the center of the hall.

'It's amazing,' I said, and the emptiness of the house and the bareness of the wooden floorboards gave a tiny, disconcerting echo.

'It's a stairway to heaven,' said Nick, 'and no one quite knows how it works.'

He took me by the hand, just as he had done the first day we met, and led me through the house. It was beautiful, cool, considered, elegant, but quite surprising. The rooms were all different shapes: oval, square, rectangular. There was something mercurial within the apparent formality of the place. It was civilized, it was felicitous, but there was also something distinctly odd about it.

I didn't want to ask the wrong questions. I didn't want to break the spell. 'Who was the architect?'

'Nobody knows,' said Nick. 'Curious, isn't it? The house was built in 1808 for a man named Nathaniel Russell. He was a merchant from Rhode Island. It cost him $80,000 – in 1808. Think of that! I love it here. If we lived in a world where our consciences could be clear and I had a wife and kids and an old mom like Whistler's mother and a dad from the *Hardy Boys*, this would be my home. There would always be fresh flowers in that bowl and, in winter, without fail, every day, a log fire burning in that grate. Listen.'

I held my breath, waiting for the stillness to break. It was like watching a fat pearl of rainwater scoot to the edge of a leaf and hang there heavily, threatening, yet failing to drop off.

Suddenly there was a startling sound. It was a woman's voice, screaming, piercing, terrified. 'Shit!'

Nick ran into the hall and bounded up the flying staircase. I ran close behind. At the top, standing by the doorway to the second-floor drawing-room was an elderly lady, smartly dressed but with a pallid, mournful face, oddly not unlike that of Whistler's mother. One hand was fluttering around her mouth, the other plucking nervously at her dress. She was struggling for breath. She saw Nick. 'Oh, Nicholas, thank God it's you!'

'What's the matter, Miss Lucas?'

'It's me,' said Theo, calling out from the middle of the drawing-room. He was lounging back on a silk-covered Empire sofa, his feet up, in his hands what turned out to be a near-priceless eighteenth-century English lyre. He was strumming it casually, like an old banjo.

'Do you know him?' asked the old lady, backing even further into the jamb of the door as she squinted nervously at the laid-back intruder.

'I'm ashamed to say I do, Miss Lucas,' said Nick with a rueful snort. 'As it happens, he's quite harmless.'

'There you are!' said Theo triumphantly. 'I was going to treat you all to a selection from *The Wizard of Oz*, but before I'd even got warmed up, this Miss Lucas here burst in and spoilt the show.'

Miss Lucas's hands fluttered around her face. 'You've no business in here, young man,' she wailed.

'What do you mean, "no business"?' said Theo indignantly, sitting up. 'Do you know who I am?'

'Stop it, Theo!'

'I am Nathaniel Russell.'

Miss Lucas looked suddenly pained and bewildered. She began running her thumbs over her fingers tremulously, as though she was crumbling small pieces of bread. 'There must be some mistake.'

'No mistake, madam,' Theo persisted. 'My family used to own this property. Indeed it was my great-great-great-grandpappy's father who built it.'

'Theo!' Nick barked at him.

Miss Lucas looked from one to the other. 'But I don't understand. You're . . .' She stalled and began taking little gulps of air.

'Yes, I sure is black, lady, black as the ace of spades. But you'll recall that the first Mr Russell made his not inconsiderable fortune in the import-export business.'

'Enough, Theo, enough.'

'And what did he import, Miss Lucas?'

The poor creature gasped and looked about her for assistance. 'Really – I—'

'Come on,' Nick commanded. 'The joke's over.'

'What was it, Miss Lucas?' Theo got to his feet and adopted a coon-like grimace. 'What was it now?'

'Rice and indigo and cotton and—'

'And slaves, Miss Lucas. And slaves! And, believe it or not, one of those slave girls and old Mr Russell they got together for a bit of jiggy-jiggy, and here I am, come to claim my inheritance.' He offered the hapless old lady a modest bow.

'That's it, Theo. Show over.'

'But it's all true,' Theo crowed cheerfully. 'He was a great man, old Nathaniel Russell, and he had impeccable taste.'

'Pay no attention to him, Miss Lucas. Hard as it is to credit, he's a friend of mine. And he thinks he's amusing.'

'Oh, I see,' she muttered, but of course she didn't at all.

'He's doing it all the time, I'm sorry to say. He was turned out of the White House when he told the tour guide he was President Reagan's childhood sweetheart.'

The lady gave a tiny, tinkly, shallow laugh and said, 'I'm so sorry. I was just taken by surprise. I didn't hear you all come in.' She took a gulp of air and calmed her fluttering hands by adjusting, straightening and smoothing the front of her dress. 'So you're together, then?'

'Yes. Yes, very much so.' Nick reassured her. 'These are colleagues of mine from Thomas Browne's. Let me introduce you. This is Kirsty Macdonald. She's from California.' We shook hands. 'And Theo Quincy you've met. He's from England originally.'

'He don't know nothing.' Theo shook his head sorrowfully and stepped forward to shake Miss Lucas firmly by the hand. 'The present Nathaniel Russell, at your service, ma'am.'

Miss Lucas knew Nick (knew him well, it transpired), liked him, admired him, trusted him, but not for a moment did she believe Theo Quincy was who Nick said he was. Deep, deep down inside her, a visceral voice told her that every word of Theo's abominable tale was true.

'Are you old friends?' I asked.

'And colleagues,' said Nick. 'We're guides here. I just do Sunday afternoons, twice a month. Miss Lucas is here almost every day.'

'I love it,' she said, beginning to breathe more easily. 'There isn't a more beautiful house in Charleston.'

'I didn't expect to find anyone here this morning,' said Nick, carefully setting the lyre back in its proper position on the sofa.

'There's only me,' said Miss Lucas. 'I've been finishing off the decoration in the music room. It's all done. Do you want to see? Wait here and I'll fix the lights.'

The moment she'd gone, Nick took Theo by the lapels. It was playful, not menacing. 'What the hell were you playing at, man?'

'I was merely doing my little bit to add a touch of *je ne sais quoi* to the gaiety of nations.'

'You might have frightened her to death.'

'I doubt it.'

Theo was right. Miss Lucas looked quite composed when she returned to fetch us. 'Follow me.' She led us along the landing, around the stairwell, to another large, fine doorway. 'Now close your eyes while I open the door. Good.' I heard her turn the doorhandle. 'Now open.'

The darkened room was ablaze with tiny pins of sparkling light. Fluted pilasters, like the icing on an ornate wedding cake, framed tall, wide mirrors the size of windows. Standing in the center of the room, and reflected to infinity in the mirrors round the walls, was a magnificent Christmas tree, covered with twinkling drops of light, decorated with gorgeous red bows, heavy with swags of silver tinsel.

I looked up at Nick and saw him transfixed. His eyes

shone, with delight, with happiness and love. He turned and saw me watching him. 'Why are you looking at me like that?'

I hesitated a moment, but he smiled at me, and as he smiled I said it. 'I know your secret.'

Chapter Four

In fact, what did I know? Nothing much. Here was a guy who got a kick out of Christmas. So what? Dr Browne got his kicks out of alcohol, Miss Haversham got hers out of William Morris, and Theo Quincy appeared to get a certain heightened satisfaction from indulging his vivid imagination and frightening old ladies. In his lecture on 'Normality and the origins of obsessive-compulsive disorder', Professor Atkins maintained: 'Enthusiasms fuel sanity; hobbies are healthy; a sustained interest is in itself sustaining. The danger comes when the enthusiasm topples into obsession, when engagement moves through engrossment to entrapment. While we may not share his fetish, the man who collects women's undergarments from the nineteenth century, and does so openly, can be reckoned to be a healthy individual whose hobby can be dignified and legitimized by being described as an interest in historical costume. When the same man starts to collect contemporary female underwear, and to do so secretly, obsession may be beginning to take hold. He does what he does because he feels driven to it, but he recognizes that his behavior is probably abnormal and consequently he may feel furtive, guilty and ashamed. His central dilemma is that his very attempts to resist the compulsion produce ever-increasing tensions and anxieties which can be relieved immediately by giving in to it. This man needs our help.'

Mr Rogers, our deputy head, had the look of a man who might need help. He was fifty-three, noticeably short, unpleasantly overweight (with definite breasts and skin the texture of a balloon that was blown up forty-eight hours ago), and quite ridiculous in the eyes of the boys because he was bald yet persisted in growing the reluctant scrub of hair at the back of his head to a sufficient length to be able to stretch a few strands of it bleakly, like slime from a sea snail, across his blotchy and crenelated dome. The effect was sufficiently disconcerting to persuade Dr Browne to exclude any close-up shots of the faculty from the school prospectus. Indeed, had a photograph of Mr Rogers appeared in a newspaper, the casual reader would have to be forgiven for taking it for granted that the person portrayed was wanted on some hideous charge – pedophilia at least, necrophilia more likely. An analyst of Prof Atkins' father's generation might have been tempted to see the poor man's appearance and manner as an almost textbook exemplification of two classic but contrary types: endomorphic (fat, stocky, weak) and cerebrotonic (restricted, self-conscious, fearful). Dr Browne knew Mr Rogers well, had done so for over thirty years, and Miss Haversham knew him even better (Theo alleged they had once been lovers), but neither of these, his oldest and closest companions, had the courage to tell him how he appeared to others. Perhaps it wasn't want of courage on their part, but misplaced kindness, or even straightforward selfishness. Mr Rogers could never have been handsome, but he could have been made presentable. As it was, he was simply a fright, the boys kept their distance, strangers shied away, so Dr Browne and Miss H could keep their friend all to themselves.

I felt uncomfortable whenever I was alone with him. He breathed noisily and his upper lip appeared perpetually peppered with little bubbles of moisture as though he suffered from a constant cold but had never discovered Kleenex. Conversation with him was an ordeal because he had the disconcerting habit of invariably repeating the last word or phrase addressed to him. Misty, this distressing condition has rather a lovely name, at least I think so. It's called echolalia. Sadly, in the unlovely Mr Rogers it was yet another trait that was far from endearing.

Time was his obsession. I might have guessed it, but he told me so himself that same Sunday. When we got back from Charleston, Nick went off to play a game of soccer with some of the boys and I made my way to the faculty room to prepare my English class for the eighth grade. Mr Rogers was standing at the mantelpiece peering closely at the back of a carriage clock. 'She is fifteen seconds out,' he muttered.

I didn't want to respond. 'Does it matter?'

'Does it matter?' he repeated, not looking round but concentrating, with passionate intensity, on the arcane workings of the clock in front of him. 'Does it matter? Absolutely. And absolutely not.'

I gave one of those halfhearted, distant little grunts that speak volumes: I'm here, I hear you, I don't want to, please leave me in peace.

Mr Rogers echoed my grunt, caught the sound if not the sense of it. 'Absolutely, because this clock, while being eighty years old, is an instrument theoretically in perfect working order, consequently I would expect, indeed require, her to work perfectly. As she doesn't, she puzzles and frustrates me and I must find a way to put her in order.' He pushed his glasses back up his nose and pressed his moist moonlike face even closer to the mechanism. 'Absolutely not, because time, of course, is an impossible concept. How long is a piece of string? That we know. How long is an hour? Sixty minutes, to be sure, but how long is sixty minutes? An eternity when you're teaching the eighth grade, the twinkling of an eye when you're out for a walk with young Mr Saint.' He suppressed a giggle. 'Isn't that right?'

I didn't react. I looked blankly at the textbook in front of me and pictured Mr Rogers' pudgy thumb and forefinger adjusting the clock's delicate balance.

'I don't know if your studies have brought you into contact with the theories of the four-dimensional space-time manifold, Miss Macdonald? Personally, I don't find they help. All I know is that clocks offer us time quite objectively, but we persist in receiving it subjectively. That's why I prefer clocks to people. They're more reliable.' He was breathing more heavily now. 'Clocks are my hobby, you know. I collect them. Only working ones, naturally. Horology is the perfect pastime for someone with an inclination towards the obsessive, all that ritualistic repetition, the winding and the checking, the fiddling and the fussing.' The more I tried not to listen to him, the more insistent his voice became. 'Magnolia Hall is all very well, but if I wasn't trapped here, I'd go to live in Copenhagen. I've visited twice. They've the world's most accurate clock there, you know. She has fourteen thousand separate parts and her mechanism works in half a million different ways. The celestial pole motion will take 25,753 years to complete a full-circle and she's accurate to within half a second in 300 years.'

I wasn't looking at him, but I sensed he was salivating as he spoke. I closed my book, a little too loudly, and gathered up my papers. 'I'd better be going.'

'Better be going. Am I boring you?' Still he didn't look up from the clock. 'Or perhaps I am disgusting you. Miss Haversham once said my lust for the celestial pole was positively obscene.' He giggled again and then made his final bid to hold my attention. 'Mr Saint is passionate about clocks, too, you know.'

'But he doesn't wear a watch,' I said. How could this odious man pretend to know my hero better than I did myself?

'Doesn't wear a watch. You noticed?'

Of course I had noticed. I loved the look of Nick's wrists, the golden skin, the tiny hairs that always seemed to catch the light. The territory between his hand and the cuff of his shirt was precious to me. And private. I studied it whenever we sat together at a table and I felt I would give too much away if I looked at him directly.

'He's a remarkable guy, our Mr Saint. No watch, and he hardly ever asks the time. He must have some internal chronometer. He never arrives late for anything. Or early. He's the only person I know who seems to accept time for what it is. I reckon real time and emotional time are the same to him. He's a phenomenon.'

I wanted to get away, but the fat fisherman had baited his hook adroitly. 'Does Mr Saint collect clocks too, then?' I asked.

'Collect clocks too, then. No, no, though his family must have done, his father or grandfather or someone. He once described one of them to me. He said it was his favorite. He pictured it perfectly, sounded to me like an eighteenth-century equation clock, possibly a Daniel

Quare, except that it struck only once a year, and then a hundred times in quick succession – unusual that, probably unique.'

'Why don't you wear a watch, Nick?' I asked him later that same evening. We were sitting on the wooden bench – Misty, like a besotted schoolgirl, I thought of it as 'our bench'! – at the top of the Dutch Garden. It was cold and getting dark, but Nick didn't seem to want to move. There was still unfinished business to be dealt with that day. We both knew it.

'I'm not sure,' he said. I felt him smile. 'Life's too short.'

'Mr Rogers was telling me about your family clock. The one that chimes only once a year.'

> 'So conscious he how short time was
> For all he planned to do within it,
> He nothing did at all, alas,
> Save note the hour – and file the minute.'

It was my turn to smile now. 'Where does that come from?'

'I don't know. My head is full of stuff – so much stuff – and I don't know where half of it comes from.'

It was much darker now. I sensed he had closed his eyes. I never closed my eyes when I was with him for fear he would disappear.

'What is it?' I said.

'This morning, in Charleston. You remember?'

'Yes.'

'You said you thought you knew my secret.'

'I'm sorry.'

'Don't say that.'

'Sorry.'

'What did you mean, Kirsty?' We hear our name in another's mouth a thousand times and never notice. Whenever Nick spoke my name, I felt my heart stand still.

'I don't know. I really don't know.' What could I say? 'It's stupid,' I stumbled. 'It's nothing.'

'If you know, if you understand, it could be everything. Say it, Kirsty. Please say it.'

I whispered the word as quietly as I could. If it was his secret, why should the night air know? 'Christmas.'

'Yes,' he said, quite urgently. He wanted more. 'Yes?'

'Christmas is very special to you, and—' I hesitated. I was lost. I knew it. He was vanishing fast. A moment ago we had been so close. Now he was on Mercury and I was adrift on Mars.

'Go on.'

'And Santa Claus, he's a sort of hero-figure to you, a kind of icon.'

Something inside him snapped, like a blind rolling up unexpectedly, except no light was let in. The darkness was complete. He turned towards me, but I couldn't see his face at all. 'Yes,' he said quite calmly. 'I'm fascinated by the myth of Santa Claus, Father Christmas, St Nicholas, call him what you will. Perhaps it's because of my name. Anyway, you're right. I collect the iconography, paintings, pictures, story books, videos, too, these days, even those damnfool glass toys that you shake to make the snow fall. I reckon it's a fairly harmless recreation, don't you?'

'Yes,' I said hopelessly.

He stood up. 'You must have been inside my room.'

'Yes,' I said. I had betrayed him, and that was that.

* * *

At Thomas Browne's, anything that happened more than once was immediately given the status of a tradition. Although the school had been in existence only since the 1970s, a calendar of events with antique names, an assortment of eccentric customs and a peculiar school jargon all helped to give the illusion that the Academy was an ancient foundation. The first English settlers had arrived in the vicinity in 1670, after all, sent out from the old country by eight fortunate aristocrats – known as the Lord Proprietors – to whom King Charles II had granted a domain that stretched from Florida to Virginia, and Dr Browne encouraged potential parents to believe that he himself was a direct descendant of one of these early settlers (which was almost true) and that his school was possibly, just possibly, the first, or certainly the second, college for young gentlemen to be established in North America (which it was not). Like the great private schools of old England – Eton, Harrow, Winchester – the Thomas Browne Academy, a fraction their age, a tenth their size, but quite their equal in pretension, was divided into 'houses'. Throughout your time at the school you owed a special allegiance to your given 'house', and your housemaster (or mistress in the case of Miss Haversham) was there as your 'mentor, moral tutor and special friend'. In England the houses might well have been named after the head of house (Haversham, Rogers, Quincy); at Thomas Browne's the headmaster's marketing instinct led him to honor the houses with the names of three of the most distinguished of Good King Charles's Lord Proprietors. Whether boy princeling from Abu Dhabi or hapless scion of a broken home in Omaha, on your first day at Thomas Browne's the Head would meet and greet you in his study and then and there decide to which house you should belong. As a rule the taller boys joined Albemarle, the shortest went to Clarendon and 'the ones I regard as particularly plain are destined for Shaftesbury. It may be arbitrary, but it works.' There was no school uniform, but you could always recognize a Browne boy: whether you were faculty or fellow student he would shake you by the left hand. 'It is the only sinister thing about us,' was the little joke the headmaster made to those few parents who were able to take time personally to accompany their offspring to Magnolia Hall at the beginning of their first semester.

If not actually in its third century, the school was at least in its third decade so that a number of the forms and customs of the place were truly well established. The Headmaster's Dinner for Good Thief Sunday was not among them. The idea had come to him only forty-eight hours earlier, he would make up the required rituals as the evening progressed, but, he sensed rightly that before the night was out, another putative tradition would have taken firm root in the folklore of the school.

'Ah, Miss Macdonald and Mr Saint, you have arrived together and, of course, on time.' We had walked from the Dutch Garden to the house without speaking. As we stepped into Dr Browne's study and his clock chimed eight, Nick seemed to all the world (and to me) his usual, gentle, engaging self. The coldness, the distance, the contained anger had all gone.

'Hamlet is himself again,' said Quincy to nobody in particular.

The headmaster pressed over-filled chilled glasses upon us. 'This is my special cocktail in honor of poor St Dismas. We don't know if he came from Barbados, but he might have done. Two shots of rum, the juice of a whole fresh lime, two good splashes of crème de menthe and a dash of Angostura bitters. I think Our Lord would have approved, don't you? After all, he promised him a place in paradise, and I reckon this little green fixer comes with the passport.'

'Why are we honoring St Dismas tonight, headmaster?' Even after all these years Miss Haversham got a small but palpable charge out of the word 'headmaster'. She took a tiny sip of the cocktail and momentarily squeezed her eyes tight shut. 'I understand his proper Feast Day is the twenty-fifth of March.' Miss Haversham had a well-worn *Dictionary of Saints*.

'The twenty-fifth of March,' repeated Mr Rogers. He turned to me and smirked, 'The traditional date of the Crucifixion.'

'I thought I'd explained at Prayers, Miss H. I'm so sorry if I forgot.' He turned towards us, hands outstretched, palms uppermost, in supplication. 'As some of you may know, the National Catholic Prison Chaplains' Association reserves the second Sunday in October as Good Thief Sunday, and I rather felt that if it was good enough for them, and since we're not all here at Easter . . .'

He left the sentence hanging in the air as he pottered over to his desk and began rummaging among his papers. 'I have the cutting here somewhere. There was a paragraph in the *Courier* on Friday. It's all *bona fide*.'

'The cocktail is most excellent, anyhow,' said Quincy, helping himself to the shaker.

'We'll be toasting Barabbas later,' muttered Dr Browne, returning to the fold empty-handed. 'That'll be the one that gives you the headache.'

Mr Rogers moved closer towards me, a film of green

cocktail glistening about his lips. 'St Dismas is the patron saint of persons condemned to death.'

'Cheerio!' called Dr Browne, retrieving and replenishing his glass.

'Not just them,' said Nick quite quietly. 'All kinds of people in prison.' Mr Rogers revealed a tip of green tongue, and retreated.

'I thought that was St Sebastian,' said Dr Browne.

Mr Quincy blew a plume of blue smoke towards the headmaster, and murmured, 'He just looks after the gay convicts, Dr B.'

Suddenly Mr Rogers was beginning to breathe quite fast. 'How about St Nicholas? He fits in here somewhere, doesn't he? Murderers and fallen women, that's his scene, isn't it?'

'And children,' I said.

'Yeah, sure,' said Quincy. 'We all know about the kids. It's the murderers and the fallen women we want to hear about. Isn't that right, Nick?'

Nick laughed. He didn't seem in the least disconcerted. 'Yes, Theo, I believe fallen women do come in to the legend. I'm surprised you're interested.'

'I thought very little of substance was known about him,' Miss Haversham interpolated primly. The lives of the saints was her sacred ground.

'You're right, Miss H, as ever.' I didn't look up at him, but his voice was warm and easy. I began to feel safe again. 'We know he was a bishop in the fourth century at a place called Lycia, in what's now North Africa.'

'My kind of country,' bubbled Quincy. 'My kind of guy.'

'That's about all anyone knows for certain, isn't it, Miss H? But there are stories galore. The one with the fallen women has him saving three girls from prostitution by throwing three bags of gold into their window at night as a dowry. That's why he's the patron saint of pawnbrokers, among others. And he shares their symbol, the three balls.'

'Three balls,' echoed Mr Rogers.

'I like it!' Quincy yelped. 'I like it!'

Miss Haversham was anxious to contribute to the hagiography. 'I do believe murder may have been involved somewhere along the line. There's a little bell ringing way in the distance. I'll have to check it out.'

'According to one of the old tales,' said Nick, 'he brought three young boys back to life after they had been murdered and hidden in a tub of brine.'

'Tub of brine. How do we know?' asked Mr Rogers.

'We don't,' said Nick. 'It's all tall stories conjured up in the mists of time. The only consistent part is the rule of three. Three girls, three boys. There were three condemned men he was supposed to have rescued and three sailors brought back to life from a watery grave. A character called Methodius began to embroider the legend in the early eight hundreds. His is the first written account.'

'Written account. You've read it?'

'No,' said Nick very simply. 'I'm relying on *Sancti Nicolae Acta Primigenia* by N.C. Falconius, 1751. It's the standard work.'

For a moment the room was quite still, then Nick burst out laughing.

'Drink up, everybody,' commanded Dr Browne, draining his glass with a sudden burst of unexpected energy. 'We mustn't keep the electric wok waiting.'

As we moved towards the table, Quincy whispered to me, 'Remember, Nick Saint never lies.'

It had been a long day, Misty, but it wasn't over yet. By eleven, Quincy and Mr Rogers were quite drunk and Miss Haversham was asleep at the table. With some ceremony, Dr Browne was preparing his nightcap. 'I call it The Pre-penultimate. It gives me hope.' We said goodnight, but no one seemed to notice us go. In the alcove outside our rooms Nick kissed me kindly on the cheek and, as I tried to speak, put his fingers up to my lips, as he had done once before.

'Don't say it. Goodnight.'

'Goodnight.'

I lay in my narrow bed, beneath the cold white quilt, gazing up at the whitewashed ceiling. The drive to Charleston, arm in arm. The flying staircase. Theo. Mr Rogers. Our bench in the Dutch Garden. Good Thief Sunday. I would never forget, never, the agony and the ecstasy.

On the chair by my bed was my traveling alarm clock. It was the old-fashioned sort that you had to wind up. Mom and Dad had given it to me one Christmas, when I was six or seven. It was my most prized possession. It had a clear, comforting tick and large, luminous hands that shone out at me like twinkling lights in a welcoming cottage set on top of a distant hill. Sometimes, at night, looking back or looking forward and wondering why so little is ever right at the time, I would take the clock and close it within its small green square case and tuck it under my pillow. I pretended the distant ticking was my mother's heart. I could always get to sleep that way.

I looked at the clock now. It was half after one. I heard a noise out on the landing, a footfall. It couldn't be one of the boys. When they came up to our floor, you heard them first scurrying along the corridor below.

Gently, noiselessly, my door began to open and I saw a tall figure, hooded and still, standing framed in the doorway, like the silhouette of a cowled monk in a stained-glass window.

'Nick, is it you?'

The figure moved towards the bed.

'Nick?'

'Can we talk?'

'Yes, Nick. I'd like that.'

He pulled back his hood. I could see the outline of his face. He looked like an exhausted child.

'What's wrong?' I turned and rested on my elbow. With my other hand I smoothed down the quilt and patted it as though he were a small boy and I was trying to tempt him to sit quietly on the corner of the rug to eat his picnic. As he sat next to me, his hand touched my wrist. Lightly, slowly, he ran his fingers, like a soft make-up brush, across my veins. He touched my pulse.

'What is it?'

'Kirsty, forgive me.'

'There's nothing to forgive.'

'What I start now, who knows where it will end?'

'What is it, Nick?'

'I want to tell you my secret.'

I was afraid. I heard the ticking of the traveling clock. 'Don't, Nick. Don't if you don't want to.'

'I want to. I have never told anyone, but now I want to tell you. I thought perhaps you'd guessed, but you hadn't. I was angry with myself, not with you.' He ran his fingers up over my wrist and gently spread out the palm of my hand as though he were straightening crumpled tissue. He traced each line and pushed the fingers slowly apart, one by one. 'Kirsty, I've never told Theo, but I want you to know. Don't be shocked; don't be frightened.' I was afraid, Misty. We are afraid of the unknown. 'I have said the words inside my head so many times. Now I've got to say them out loud, it isn't easy.'

'Just whisper.'

'Kirsty, dearest friend, it's just this. I believe, I don't quite know how, but I believe that I am, or I have been, or I will be—' he hesitated, then he said it – 'Santa Claus – Father Christmas – St Nicholas, call him what you like. I know it's absurd, childish, irrational. It makes no sense, and yet it is the only thing that does make sense. It's what I believe. It's who I am. And now you know.'

He laid his face on my hand and I felt the warm tears trickle into my palm.

Chapter Five

'He thinks he's fucking Santa Claus!' The roll of laughter was like a rumble of thunder all the way from Monterey. 'Christ almighty, babe, what kind of weirdo is he? What kind of place is it?'

'It's just a school,' I said. 'He's just a guy.' Why had I called Professor Atkins? Why had I no one else to call?

'Are you in love?'

'I think so. I'm not sure.'

'Is he in love with you?'

Vanity made me hesitate. 'No. No, but – I think he needs me.'

'Oh yeah?'

'I think he's gay.' Another roll of mocking laughter rumbled across the land.

'Don't laugh, Prof.'

'My child, I laugh that I may not weep!'

'Maybe he's not gay; maybe he's nothing.'

'Jesus, Kirsty, I can't believe I'm hearing this.'

'He's kind, he's generous, he's good.'

'And if he thinks he's fucking Santa Claus, he's nuts. Get out, babe, cut loose. Now.'

'I can't, Prof.'

'Don't give me that bullshit. There's no such word as

can't and you know it. This thing will end in tears – as sure as Jung was right and Freud was wrong!'

'You don't understand.'

'Try me.'

I told him the whole story. He listened attentively, and when he broke in with questions – 'Does he have hallucinations? Does he hear voices? What are his mood swings? Is he secretive? Is he suspicious of you?' – his voice sounded deeper, more intimate, and at the same time muffled, as though he'd tucked the telephone under his beard. His tone was caring but professional, kindly but dispassionate. I wondered if he was taking notes.

Elaborately, noisily, the clock struck nine. 'I've got to go. I've got a class.'

'I'll call you back, babe. Give me your number.'

'No, let me call you.' I was in Dr Browne's study, using his phone. (I had told him my sister was sick. He had not asked for an explanation, but I insisted on giving one and then elaborating on it. Not content simply with inventing an ailing sibling, I felt compelled to give her a name, age, appearance, foibles, future, boyfriend, symptoms. One lie was not enough.)

'We need to talk, sweetheart. Remember Jesus Jones? Call me.'

I spent the next hour with three of our brightest seventeen-year-olds ostensibly deconstructing Robert Frost while actually reconstructing the case of Jesus Jones.

> 'Part of the moon was falling down the west
> Dragging the whole sky with it to the hills.'

I had never met JJ – that's what Professor Atkins usually called him. The Prof hadn't met him either, but JJ's wife had been one of his patients back in the sixties and 'the tragic case of Jesus Jones' was invariably quoted as the Prof's 'textbook example' of paranoid schizophrenia.

JJ was Mexican, a carpenter, a serious craftsman, in his mid-twenties, above average in intelligence, below it in height, but good-looking and supremely fit. A loner, apparently without a family, he came to San José looking for work and met Luisa; she was a waitress, about twenty-two, pretty, dark, naive; after just six weeks he married her. At first, the marriage seemed ideal. Luisa, who had lost both her parents when she was in her teens, had never been so happy. Jesus was warm and generous, assiduous in his work, considerate at home. He liked reading, he spent a lot of time at the library. He wasn't outgoing, but to Luisa he was 'kind and sexy'. Then one day, when they had been married for about eight months and were beginning to talk about having a baby, quite abruptly he changed. At first he was tetchy, argumentative, volatile, then, just as suddenly, he became aloof, remote, hard. Physically, his appearance altered. She said he began to look like a waxwork of himself. His manner became unnaturally formal, his gestures artificial, his gait deliberate, his speech contrived. When he looked at Luisa he seemed to be looking through her, like a child playing a game where the one who outstares the other is the winner. One night, when he got home from work, he told her that their life together would have to change. He explained that they should no longer have sex and that he wanted her to shower at least four times each day. He told her that she was unclean and that uncleanliness was the work of the devil. That's when she went to her doctor, and he referred her on to the Prof. She was bewildered, frightened, lost, alone.

'Home is the place where, when you
    have to go there,
They have to take you in.'
'I should have called it
Something you somehow haven't to deserve.'

The Prof suggested she bring JJ in to see him. He wouldn't come. He was hearing voices now. Joan of Arc told him that he must take his sword and rid the world of all its impurities. Mary, the Mother of God, told him that he was her son, the reincarnation of Jesus, Christ reborn, the Messiah returned. He had a mission to fulfill. His voices instructed him to cleanse all mankind, to search the earth and cut out the heart of darkness wherever it should be found. The Prof alerted the police, but it was too late. When they arrived at the apartment they found Luisa's body on the bed. JJ had used his chisel and a tenon-saw to cut out her heart. They found him in the kitchen, covered with blood, sitting quite calmly, sipping herb tea and annotating a copy of *The Courage to Be* by Paul Tillich. It was one of two books he had stolen from the library. The other was *Reverence for Life* by Albert Schweitzer.

'Nick Saint is no Jesus Jones.'

'I'm not saying he is, not for a moment.'

'What are you saying then, Prof?'

'I'm not saying anything, except that to go around claiming to be Santa Claus ain't normal.'

'I thought "normal" wasn't a term we used these days, Prof.'

'Come on, Kirsty babe, let's not play games. You're falling for a guy you know nothing about, and I reckon he may need help. That's all.'

Misty, sometimes there is nothing so infuriating as being

confronted with the truth. I did not know what to say.

'Kirsty?' He knew I was still there. I had nowhere else to turn and, after all, he was giving me what I had called for. I had run towards him like a frightened child and he had taken me in his arms, but now I wouldn't be comforted, I wouldn't be grateful. I had called him feeling vulnerable and confused and his very strength and certainty had made me feel exposed and foolish – and angry, angry at my own weakness and naivete, and angry with him for being exactly what I needed him to be: mature, kindly, wise. My silence was sullen and resentful. Like a seasoned father, he ignored it. 'Kirsty,' he said, with deliberate authority, 'I've spoken to David Hofmann. If you can get your young man to go to New York, he'll see him – no charge. Okay?'

I said 'Okay', took the details, replaced the telephone and stood gazing blankly out the window towards the cedar grove.

'The best way out is always through.'

Startled, I turned to find Dr Browne standing at my shoulder. 'Sorry?' Abruptly I was brought back from a faraway land.

'My favorite line of Robert Frost,' he said, holding up my copy of the poems. 'Great man. We share a birthday. Different years, of course.' He giggled softly and tilted his head to one side. 'And how is your poor dear sister?'

'It may be a tumor,' I said gravely. 'They're not sure.'

He turned the book over in his dainty, well-scrubbed hands. 'This is a neat edition.' He handed it back, as though he were giving me a present. 'Have you ever read *The Importance of Being Earnest*?'

'No.'

'You should,' he chuckled. 'You'd like it.' He began to straighten the papers on his desk. 'So you'll go visit your sister in the mid-semester break?'

'Yes.'

'Good,' he said. 'In New York?'

'Yes,' I said, 'in New York.'

In *The Politics of Experience*, R.D. Laing is emphatic: 'It seems to us that *without exception* the experience and behavior that gets labeled schizophrenic is *a special strategy that a person invents in order to live in an unlivable situation.*' He is sanguine, too: 'Madness need not be all breakdown. It may also be break-through. It is potential liberation and renewal as well as enslavement and existential death.' I needed to justify Nick, what he was, what he might be. And I wanted hope. Rather pathetically, I also wanted to justify myself, what I was doing, what I was going to do.

In *Self and Others*, Laing says: 'True guilt is guilt at the obligation one owes to oneself to be oneself. False guilt is guilt felt at not being what other people feel one ought to be or assume that one is.'

Sitting that night on the edge of Nick's bed, the guilt I felt was of a less equivocal and more prosaic nature. I was letting myself fall in love with a man and allowing myself to deceive him at the same time. It didn't feel too good.

'Do you think I'm mad?' He was lying flat on his back, with his hands behind his head. It was a serious question, but he asked it playfully.

'No.'

'Then why do you want me to see your shrink?' He smiled.

'Because he might help?'

'How? I've checked the textbooks. My condition doesn't feature.'

Misty, I can't tell you how beautiful this man was.

Looking at him lying on his narrow bed, the tousled golden head against the bright white pillow, I thought if Sleeping Beauty had been a guy, this is the guy he'd have been.

I brushed the hair off his forehead. He watched me, amused. Slowly he moved his hand, I thought to take mine. In fact, he stretched out his arm and reached for the tiny Santa that was hanging from a branch of his Christmas tree. He cupped the little figure tenderly in his hand and then flicked it so that it spun, first rapidly round one way then back more slowly round the other.

'I know everything there is to know about Santa Claus, everything. From the legend of old Saint Nick and his sidekick Black Peter through Dasher and Dancer and Donner and Blitzen, I've read it all, seen it all, lived and breathed it all – but it's make-believe, isn't it? What do I know about *me*? Nothing. All I am, all that I *know* I am, is an ordinary guy with an extraordinary obsession – an obsession so extraordinary, so fantastic, so childish, so *dumb*, that in twenty-eight years I've only dared share it with one other human being. I'm in no-man's-land, Kirsty, and I don't know the way out.'

'Maybe Dr Hofmann could help you find a way out, a way through.'

'How?'

'By taking you back to the beginning. We can't know where we are till we know where we've come from.'

He turned on his side and half sat up, leaning on his arm, watching the little Santa come to rest. 'Recovered memories, that kind of stuff?'

'Yes.' I didn't want to sound too eager.

'I tried it once. With Theo. Years ago. I hadn't been here long. I was twenty or twenty-one. We shared a room then. In the main house. It was before this wing was done up. In those days Theo was into drugs in a big way, and one New Year – he'd been away, up in Chicago – he came back, all excited. You know Theo. "I've got this truth serum," he announced. "Why don't we try it? Unlock our secret selves." It was sodium amytal. He said it was harmless, that all we had to do was take it and talk. "Happy-happy-talk."'

'Did it work?'

'I've got the tape somewhere. You can judge for yourself. We set it up like a scientific experiment. The idea was that one night Theo would give me the shot and ask all the questions and the next night it would be his turn. I had only one question I wanted him to ask: What is your earliest memory?'

'And what was it?'

'Kirsty, do you really want to know?'

'Yes, Nick, I really want to know.'

'It was very simple. There wasn't much to it, but it was all quite clear. I remembered being placed in a crib filled with straw, surrounded by huge angels with golden wings, and watched over by two figures, one hooded with a white beard, the other all in black.'

We flew in to New York on Monday afternoon and checked in at the Chelsea Hotel, 222 West 23rd Street. Apparently the Thomas Browne Academy for Boys had some sort of deal going with the Chelsea, a special rate for members of faculty, out of season. The notion seemed less improbable the moment I got out of the cab and looked up at the building, twelve floors of faded Gothic grandeur, ornate pillars, elaborate iron balconies, fearsome dormer windows, capped with grand guignol gables that would have made Nathaniel Hawthorne's heart skip a beat. The huge vertical neon sign that spelt out the hotel's name added to the sense of unreality. I felt I was arriving on the decaying backlot of a once celebrated movie studio. When I climbed the steps and crossed the threshold I wouldn't have been surprised to find that behind the monstrous façade there was nothing there.

In fact there was plenty. Too much. The front desk was besieged by newly-arrived but not-to-be-put-upon-for-a-moment graduates of the University of the Third Age, Ohio, already regretting they hadn't paid that little bit extra to stay at the St Regis. The lobby itself was a blaze of light: TV arc lamps shone down on a bewildered huddle of punk rockers waiting to be interviewed. It seemed our visit was coinciding with the anniversary of one of the more notorious episodes in the Chelsea's colorful history: the stabbing to death in Room 100 of a young woman named Nancy Spungen, a Philadelphia groupie and girlfriend of Sid Vicious, prince of punk and star of the Sex Pistols. Twenty years on, in a live telecast, ABC were still asking the same question: did Sid Vicious do it?

New York I knew hardly at all. Nick knew it well. Even in the cab I could tell he was exhilarated to be back. 'I've no idea where I was born, but Brooklyn is where I was brought up, and as a kid I'd take the subway to Penn Station and spend hour after hour just walking the streets of Manhattan. This is my part of town.' The cab was jerking us slowly down Sixth Avenue. 'Look, on the corner, "Lox Around the Clock". Do you like bagels?'

'I love bagels.'

'We shall have bagels at midnight and count the stars!'

'Can you see the stars in New York?'

'In Chelsea you can. In Chelsea anything is possible! There's magic in the air in Chelsea.'

I laughed. Looking down the streets that we passed the buildings seemed to alternate between tacky tenement blocks of indeterminate age and flat-fronted apartment houses, concrete monuments to the banality of the 1950s. Here and there a homely turn-of-the-century town-house spoke (faintly) of a more elegant era, but, at least at first glance, it was hard to visualize this drab district as an oasis of enchantment.

'I was about twelve or thirteen when I first discovered these streets. God knows what drew me here. In its heyday this stretch of Sixth Avenue was home to every kind of vice: it was Times Square with added temptation! There were movie houses and dance halls all along here. By all accounts, a hundred years ago this is the place where America was introduced to the can-can and where, if you wanted them, you could find pimps and prostitutes under every lamppost. They still call it Satan's Circus.'

At the hotel, thankfully, we were not offered Room 100. We had a small suite on the floor above, with a shared bathroom connecting a pair of identical bedrooms, each predictably furnished, drab but conventionally welcoming, like a nondescript *maître d'* you never expect to see again.

Nick began unpacking at once. 'Is this going to be okay?'

'It's great,' I said. Why am I lying all of a sudden? I hate it here. It's tacky. We shouldn't have come.

I caught sight of myself in the wardrobe mirror. I felt I was seeing a stranger. I mouthed the words: 'Is it really you?' Out loud I said, 'Do you think anyone was murdered in this room?'

'Dylan Thomas is supposed to have died here,' Nick said cheerfully, 'but I doubt if it was in this suite. They'd have charged extra.'

I stood quite still, slowly examining my appearance in the mirror, trying to get reacquainted. I could hear Nick in his room, moving about, unpacking his bag, busy, contented.

'Did you ever see *The Chelsea Girls*?'

'The Andy Warhol movie? No.'

'You look a bit like Edie Sidgwick, that's all. Just the eyes.' He was standing in the doorway now. 'Only kidding.'

'Who's Edie Sidgwick?'

'One of the ghosts of the Chelsea.' He moved back into the bathroom and began unpacking his spongebag. 'She was in the movie; she was a kind of Warhol groupie, but he got tired of her in the end and moved on.'

'Did he murder her?'

Nick laughed. 'Not quite. Poor Edie . . . As Theo would say, "She did not treat her body as a temple." She was one of the barbiturate babes of the swinging sixties. She let the good times roll and ended up here at the Chelsea living on a diet of potato salad and amphetamine-flavored coffee. Legend has it she nearly burned the hotel down – twice. Came from a good family, Boston belle, social register, all the rest. Who knows what went wrong? Too much money, too much ambition, not enough love. Was it the world in general or the Sidgwicks in particular? I've a theory that something strange happened to the planet in the second half of the nineteen-sixties, but, even so, this was not a lucky family. She had two brothers, and all three of them spent time in institutions of one kind or another.'

I moved towards the bathroom. The light was brighter there. 'What happened to the brothers?'

'They died too.'

'God. Were they murdered?'

'No.' Nick smiled. 'Suicide, both of them.' He laid his toothbrush on the shelf and looked at me in the bathroom mirror. 'Dr Hofmann didn't get to them in time.'

My arms were folded. I looked down at them. It was almost eight o'clock. I looked up at Nick. 'And?'

'And so it came to pass that little elfin Edie, the petite, cute, wide-eyed wild child, moved from Massachusetts to New York and, one fine night, found herself at a party, face to face with the icon of the era, Mr Andy Warhol no less. She was smitten, so was he. She cut off her hair, spiked it up, dipped the tips in silver, and turned herself into a kind of weird Warhol look-alike. She was famous, and for more than fifteen minutes. She got almost a whole year in the limelight – Andy and Edie were an item. Then, one day, they weren't. And, not so long after, she was dead.'

'Have you got any other cheerful little tales to tell me?'

Nick put his comb into his coat pocket and turned towards me. 'Sorry.' He kissed me lightly on the cheek. There was familiarity without intimacy, as though I were his oldest friend's newly-acquired second wife. 'Thoughtless. I'll leave you in peace. Let you unpack. I want to go to the library anyway. There's just time. I need to check out something. I won't be long. Be good.'

He went. I checked the lock on the bathroom door. I didn't unpack. I couldn't. I called Room Service. I wanted to hear another voice. For nearly three hours I sat almost motionless on the edge of the bed, drinking coffee that got progressively colder and watching TV that got progressively more meaningless as, almost without pause, I flicked relentlessly from channel to channel. I had questions and no answers, not even the beginnings of answers snuffling, shuffling, whimpering towards me. Nothing. Who is he? Who is Nick Saint? And how the hell have I ended up alone in New York sharing a shabby suite with a man I don't know and can't begin to make out? 'Whatever you do, don't fall in love with him. That way madness lies.'

I heard his key in the lock. 'Kirsty.' The door closed abruptly behind him. 'Kirsty, come here, would you?' He sounded different.

'What is it?' I thought I couldn't move. So this is being petrified?

'I want to show you something.' He said it urgently.

I stood up. My spine was numb, my thighs ached. As I turned, I was startled by the stranger in the mirror. I stared back at her pallid, fearful face.

'Kirsty!' I walked through the bathroom. I'd left the doors wide open, the lights full on.

Nick looked different. His face was white. He was trembling, just slightly, as though he were cold. He gazed straight at me.

'Did you know it was a trap?'

'What are you talking about?'

'Did you know it was a trap?' he repeated.

'What are you saying?'

'I am asking you about Dr Hofmann.'

'I don't know what you're saying.' But now, of course, I did.

'Don't you, Kirsty? Well, I'll tell you.' He held a piece of paper in his hand. He waved it at me. 'This is a Xerox of a page from *Who's Who in America*. It contains a fairly extensive biography of a certain Dr David Hofmann. If the address is to be believed, it would appear to be your Dr Hofmann, "our" Dr Hofmann, the friendly shrink-next-door I'm scheduled to hand myself over to at nine o'clock tomorrow morning – unless, of course, there are two eminent psychiatrists of the same name who just happen to share an office. What's so odd about this Dr Hofmann is that in his long list of scholarly accomplishments there appears to be no mention of his celebrated work on the recovered memory syndrome. On the contrary, this distinguished gentleman's curriculum vitae makes it crystal clear that he is one of America's most sought-after *forensic* psychiatrists. It seems he has given over his life to the detailed study of the criminal mind and is acknowledged as our great nation's foremost authority on every aspect of paranoid schizophrenia. I call this the second betrayal!'

With both arms he took hold of me so that the piece of paper was crushed against my shoulder. 'Open your eyes.' His voice was different. 'Please open your eyes.' Misty, he said it with such gentleness that, quite suddenly, I wasn't frightened any more. His beautiful blue eyes were smiling. 'Kirsty, I am not mad. I may be different, but I am not mad. Trust me. Please trust me.'

Outside, a long way off, a clock began to strike twelve. 'Come on,' he whispered. 'I promised you a bagel.'

Chapter Six

'If I'm not the original Santa Claus, and I understand your reservations, Kirsty – I respect them – Lord knows, I have my own – and I'm not a paranoid schizophrenic on the loose – and I'm truly grateful to you for giving me the benefit of the doubt on that one – the question is: who the hell am I?'

Nick Saint was himself again. In his fantastic bathrobe (red toweling, white trimming) he was pacing between our rooms, hot coffee in one hand, crumbly croissant in the other. He stepped up on to my bed and stood over me, swaying, arms outstretched.

'Well?'

'Don't spill the coffee!'

Feet planted either side of me, he bounced gently up and down. 'I shall scald you like a psychopath.' He held the coffee cup over my head and tipped it slowly towards me. I squealed and made for the covers. 'All gone. Blast!' he said, twirling the empty cup on his index finger like a toy six-shooter. 'I'm having more. How about you?' He jumped off the bed and went to top up the coffee.

'I'm fine.' I felt it. 'I feel wonderful.' Full of wonder I surely was. For a start, the hotel room, alien and so cramped and bleak last night, was now a nest, cosy, comfortable. I stretched out my legs and luxuriated in the easy warmth of the bed, the uncomplicated sensation of fresh linen on clean skin. My toes caught hold of one of the studs on the edge of the quilt.

'I'd hate to be a mermaid,' I said.

'You'd make a great mermaid. The best.'

I sat up and threw a pillow at him. He dropped his coffee on the tray, caught the pillow mid-air and threw it right back, hard. With a roar, he ran at the bed and bounced on to it with his knees; he grabbed the other pillow and began battering my head with it. I rolled to the right, off the bed, and raced through the bathroom to his bedroom. I caught hold of one of his pillows and holding it tight in both fists swung it high above my head. Now we were both armed. Buff. Biff. Paff. Kerpow! Over beds, onto chairs, we hurtled from one room to the next in a wild, enchanted chase, swinging our pillows, slamming, banging, thumping, thwacking, yelling, laughing, screaming, yelping, until we collapsed, in an exhausted, exhilarated heap, back where we had started.

Nick was panting hard. I climbed on top of him and, rapt in love, gazed down at my glorious blue-eyed boy. I let my elbows rest either side of his head and with both my hands pushed his hair back off his forehead. I did it quite severely, as though I was an old-fashioned governess giving her young charge's head a proper brushing.

I pushed my face right down towards his. '*Who are you*, Nick Saint?'

From behind me his arms came up and he took hold of my shoulders and pulled me gently back as he sat up. Our faces were almost touching. He ground his teeth, snarled softly and mock-made to bite off my nose. Hannibal Lecter meets Holly Golightly. He was grinning from ear to ear. 'I have no idea. I have *no* idea, little Miss Mac.' He pushed me over onto the bed, reached out and picked up a pillow off the floor and buried me under it.

I pulled the pillow away from my face. He wasn't looking towards me now. He was staring intently at the vacant TV screen, peering into some dark unfathomable pool of his own imagining.

'Don't you have a birth certificate?' I asked.

'Christ, no.'

'Hospital records?'

'Not that I'm aware of.'

'Passport?'

'I'm not planning to leave the country, since you ask. Theo tried to persuade me to come on a trip to Canada once, but I wouldn't risk it. To acquire a passport you need a birth certificate. About ten years ago I spent six weeks of eight-hour days at the census bureau, checking out every Saint in the land. Eventually it dawned on me that Nicholas Saint is most unlikely to be my real name anyway.'

'What about a driving license?'

'I don't have one. I just drive very carefully.'

'Won't you get arrested?'

'Who would they charge?' He turned towards me and took my hands in his. 'Yes, my supercharged friend, I'm the man who isn't here. Even the IRS haven't gotten on to me.'

I let go of him and pulled up my knees. 'What's your earliest memory?'

'I told you.'

'That doesn't count,' I said. 'That could have been a fantasy. Nick – whoever you are, whatever you're called – think. Think carefully. Something must come first. Think about it. What is it? Go back, flick through the book, flick right through, get back to page one. What's the picture? Don't imagine it. See it. What is it? What's your own, your very own first recollection, something in your head now that's as real as it was then, something you can touch, hold, feel, know is yours and no one else's, real and true and substantial.'

He looked towards the TV again and then turned back towards me. 'Walking along the Boardwalk,' he said, 'with Sister Peta holding my hand. We each had a chocolate malted. I can hear the funny slurpy sound hers made when she got to the end and went on sucking through her straw.'

'Who's Sister Peta?'

'One of the nuns. At the kids' home. On Coney Island.'

'Okay, let's start there.'

The world divides, Misty, into those for whom the terrible tackiness of Coney Island has a hypnotic charm, and those high-minded unsentimental souls for whom it doesn't. As you can guess, the moment I set eyes on the place I was hooked. The straggling stretch of pleasure beach, deserted and fly-blown; the forlorn Ferris wheel, evidently once the glory of its age; the clanking roller-coasters with gorgeous names (the Thunderbolt, the Cyclone, the Whip, the Mile Sky Chaser, the Comet, the Flying Turns); the mighty Parachute Jump, now abandoned, in 1939 the very wonder of the World's Fair; the rows of touchingly optimistic stalls offering clams you don't quite trust, ice-cream, iced beer, meretricious beach toys and plastic sun glasses out of season; the mysterious booths where, in four minutes or less, you can have your portrait sketched or your fortune foretold or your checks cashed (at a price): this was the playground of the people, 'the empire of the nickel', now bereft of promise, well past its prime, but to me, immediately and profoundly compelling.

'I like it,' I said, *con brio*.

'You're sweetly sentimental for an analyst,' said Nick, with a sideways glance and an indulgent smile.

'I'm a therapist,' I said. 'We're different.' He lifted his eyebrows in an affectation of disdain and lengthened his stride. 'Where are we going?'

'To the end of the road.' We had taken the B line to the Stilwell Avenue stop and were now walking briskly along Surf Avenue, stalking past idling day-trippers and knots of kids without purpose, as though they were cardboard cutouts, merely there to dress the set, while we, the real people, marched boldly through. 'We are on our way to the Convent of the Sacred Heart.'

'The kids' home?'

'My only home. Six Irish nuns, twenty little orphan Annies and one Nicholas Saint.'

'God, that explains everything!'

'I thought you said you therapists were different.'

'*Touché*.' I laughed. 'How old were you when you left?'

'Seventeen. They weren't supposed to keep boys beyond ten, but they didn't know where to send me, so a unique dispensation was given in my case. I was their "special blessing", their golden child, not just destined for the priesthood, destined for the top.'

We turned right into Gravesend Reach.

'Sister Peta used to call me her "little man of destiny". God help me, for years I believed her! She used to say,

"He'll be the first American pope, I know it, and when he is he'll have us all over to Rome for vacations." She was full of dreams, Sister Peta. How I loved her. She wasn't like the other nuns. She was big and loud and laughed all the time. She had a round face and rosy cheeks and she used to say, "Don't I look just the spitting image of my hero now?" And guess who her hero was? It wasn't His Holiness, I'm afraid, or Cardinal Spellman, or even J.F.K.' He stopped in his tracks and looked at me with obvious delight at the sheer pleasure of the recollection. 'It was Oscar Wilde. She worshipped Oscar Wilde. She called him "St Oscar". She read us the fairy tales and the poems and she produced her own version of *The Happy Prince* one Christmas instead of a nativity play. Everyone was deeply shocked.'

'Why didn't you keep in touch?'

'I did. I do.' He paused again, and looked up at the shattered windows of what seemed to be a disused warehouse. 'When I left, I wrote every week, and then every month, but she wrote back only twice – postcards, pictures of Dublin – and then not at all. I kept on writing for two or three years and then I thought, what's the point? I still send her a card at Christmas and Easter, and on Oscar Wilde's birthday, but it's more than ten years since I had any contact. To tell you the truth, I'm a little scared of seeing her again.'

'How old will she be?'

'If she's alive . . . I don't know. Sixty-five, seventy. She was like a mother to me.' We crossed the street and looked back at the warehouse. 'What's this bull-shit I'm giving you? I don't know what a mother's like because I haven't had one. All I can say is she was special.' Suddenly with a clenched fist he punched his palm. 'But I don't believe you're going to get to meet her.'

'Why not?'

'Because the convent isn't here.'

'What do you mean?'

'That's where it was.' He indicated the warehouse. 'And there, next door—' he pointed to an ugly brown brick and limestone edifice, a squat and shabby office block – 'that used to be the playground. It's all gone, vanished.'

The nondescript buildings looked real enough, quite old too. 'It can't have done,' I protested.

'But it has,' he said, puzzled. 'It was there and now it isn't.'

'Maybe you imagined it.'

'Maybe.' He turned away, turned back the way we had come. He seemed suddenly relieved to be going back, grateful, perhaps, to have been spared a difficult encounter. He put his arm through mine. 'Well, Kirsty, this is Coney Island. You can't leave Coney Island without visiting the Aquarium, it's world famous, the oldest aquarium in North America. In my day they had real mermaids there. Let's see if they've gone and vanished too.'

'Fuck 'em, they have!'

Some of the greatest glories of the deep were on display at the Aquarium that afternoon – sharks and stingray, squirrelfish and flounder, octopuses from the Pacific, moray eels from the Caribbean, even the legendary Queen triggerfish from the Bermuda Triangle – but no mermaids, not one. The closest we got to it, I reckon, was a glimpse of the fantastic unicorn tang, with its dangling proboscis, Jagger-like lips and vast protuberant eyes, more merman than mermaid.

'Did you come here a lot as a kid?'

'All the time. I spent hours on end in the penguin rookery. Sister Peta hated it. Said it was too much like the convent. Her favorites were the sea turtles, for the laughs. And the piranhas, for the action.'

'Look,' I said, nodding in the direction of the crowd gathering at the entrance to the Aquatheatre (where a walrus met The Carpenters every half hour), 'is that her over there?' Two nuns, one little, one large, like Brobdingnagian escapees from the penguin rookery, were busy shepherding a group of small kids into line.

Nick became quite still. The glance he gave them was almost furtive. 'No,' he said. 'No,' and he put his hand out to restrain me.

'Come on,' I persisted. 'Let's see if they know her. It can't do any harm.'

Nick half-turned away as I ran over to the nuns. The line was starting to move. 'Excuse me,' I said, too loudly, as though I was on the platform calling out to passengers on a departing train. 'You don't either of you happen to know a Sister Peta, do you? She was at the Convent of the Sacred Heart. She's an old friend . . .'

'I'm sorry,' said the older nun; she was the larger one, heavy with indignation as much as anything else. She looked away as she spoke. 'I'm so sorry.' Her words weren't addressed to me, but to the world in general. She appeared to be apologizing for allowing this intrusion. Cloaking her outrage in professionalism, she marshaled her flock up the ramp to see the show. The smaller, younger, sister, who had appeared quite bewildered by my approach, now avoided my eye altogether and began hushing the kids who were chirruping and twittering like baby Beluga whales. The party quickly reached the top of the ramp and disappeared. I turned back to Nick. He had gone. I stood for a moment looking round the mall, trying to locate him, when the young nun came running back down the ramp towards me. 'Here,' she said. 'Call here, this is where she works.' She handed me a scrap of paper on which she had scrawled a number: 718 768 DYKE.

I found Nick back with the black-footed penguins. 'If you won't call, I will.'

'I'll call,' he said.

'Now?'

'Why not?' We found a phone and dialled the number. I could hear the clear, strong voice that answered. 'The Lesbian Herstory Archives. How can I help you?'

Nick hesitated. 'I'm trying to get hold of an old friend, and I've been given your number . . .'

'Nicholas, is that you? Is that really you?'

'Sister Peta, my God! Hi! How amazing! How are you?' He was like a surprised child, excited, exultant, overwhelmed.

'Where are you?'

'At the Aquarium.'

'God, not with those penguins, I hope?' She began laughing. 'Nicholas, this is so good, *so* good. I can't believe it's you. It was meant. It must have been meant. I want to see you. I want so much to see you. Are you free today? Now? Look, I finish at quarter after five. Come round to my place at six. The vodka and blinis are on me. It's 990 Carroll Street, the top apartment. 990, have you got that? Bosie and I will be waiting for you.'

Bosie turned out to be a German sausage dog. Sister Peta turned out to be a handsome woman in her early fifties, big-boned, round-faced, rosy-cheeked as promised, but unexpectedly dark and svelte as well, more k d lang than Oscar Wilde. She opened her arms to Nick and hugged him like a hostage released, or the prodigal son returned. She held him and swayed from side to side, her eyes squeezed tight shut. 'My little man of destiny. It is so good, so *good* to see you – and your friend, she's cute.' Her look wasn't appraising. It was warm, open, genuinely welcoming. 'I'm so glad you've brought her to meet me, so glad. What are you called, darling girl? Nicholas was like a son to me, you know.' While she looked at me, she kept holding onto him as if to prove he was really there, or to make sure that, now he was, he wasn't going to disappear. 'I think about you every day, Nicholas, you know, every single day, and here you are. At last. Let me fix your drinks. This is just *so* good. I'm dazzled.'

She led us through the tiny apartment without drawing breath and, in the kitchen, handed us small silver tumblers, ice-cold, filled to the brim with neat vodka. 'Look, I've kept all your cards, every one.' They were lined up on top of her kitchen cupboards and stretched the length of the room. 'The one for Oscar's birthday only got to me on Friday. They come via two forwarding addresses so they always reach me about three weeks late, but he never lets me down, he never forgets his Sister Peta. You've not forgotten once, Nicholas, not once. God bless you! It is so good that you're here.' She plunged her hand into his hair and held onto him. 'So good.'

'Why didn't you write back?' In the way he said it there was no hint of reproach.

She sighed, quite theatrically, and went to draw the bottle of vodka out of the ice-box. She gave herself a second shot. 'I couldn't. I just couldn't. You can see that now, can't you? You didn't know it, but you were sending letters to someone who didn't exist anymore. You were writing to Sister Peta and I wasn't that Sister Peta any longer. I couldn't write back. I didn't dare. I didn't want to shatter your illusions. I didn't want to shock you. I didn't want to hurt you. And I didn't want to lose you. God knows, I didn't want to lose you. I loved you as much as ever, but I was frightened because I knew that the person you loved had vanished altogether and I was scared that, once you knew that, your love might evaporate too. I thought, can you love someone who isn't there? A couple of times I sat down and tried to write you a proper letter explaining everything, but since I didn't really understand it all myself, I didn't get very far. I settled for a couple of postcards and I suppose I hoped you'd settle for your memories. Maybe I was wrong. Who can say? At the time, it seemed the right thing to do, the only thing to do. I was so mixed up anyway.'

'What happened?'

'What happened?' She took another drink. 'Judy Chicago's dinner party. That's what happened. Do you remember?' She was asking both of us. 'It was the beginning of the eighties, you were still at the convent, it must have been your last year. It was a great big scandal at the time. Such a fuss, such an outcry. Ridiculous, really, but it changed my life.'

We looked blank.

'It was an art show at the Brooklyn Museum, a veritable *cause célèbre*. Judy wanted to reinterpret the Last Supper "from the point of view of those who have done the cooking throughout history". It was just a brilliant idea, thirty-nine ceramic plates, featuring the heads of famous women and – wait for it, schlock, horror! – crafted like female genitalia! The papers were full of it, the outrage was everywhere, Brooklyn Heights was up in arms. Thanks to the brouhaha, there were lines round the block and, one day, I decided to join them. Yeah, a nun at Judy Chicago's dinner party. It was the beginning of the end for me – and the end of the beginning. That show was my call to action. I went back to the convent and told Sister Benedict – you remember her, you can't have forgotten her? I said, I've got to get out. I haven't lost my faith, but I've lost my way. I said, I need to break free, cut loose, find out who I am, discover my sexuality. Can you imagine, Nicholas, I used the word "sexuality" in front of Sister Benedict? Jesus! She was shocked, I could tell, alarmed too, but she kept her cool. She told me it was just a mid-life crisis. I told her it was a glorious awakening. She said wait, think, pray. I owed her a great deal, in many ways I owed the Sacred Heart everything, so I did all she asked, but the longer I waited, the harder I thought, the more I prayed, the clearer it became to me that I couldn't spend the rest of my life cooped up in a convent on Coney Island. I had to get out – and I had to come out. I waited nine months, like a proper gestation, then one wonderful day in May I gave birth to the new me. I simply took off the veil, packed my bags and walked out. It had seemed so difficult, so impossible, but when it came to it, it turned out to be easy. At least for me. It caused quite a row at the convent. And it hurt a lot of people. But it was the right thing to do. No regrets.' She drained her tumbler. 'No more vodka either. I'm high enough just seeing the two of you. This is *so* good.' She put her arms round both of us and pressed our heads to her shoulders, as though we had been nursery-rhyme children, lost in the wood and now miraculously recovered. 'Oh, shit,' she said, 'the blinis. I forgot the blinis!'

She broke away and opened the fridge. 'And let's have one more vodka each. This is a special occasion, for heaven's sake. And then let's have dinner. I'll take you to my favorite restaurant.' She looked serene, and, Misty, it wasn't just the alcohol. She knew that Nick had accepted her completely, easily, at once. He loved her still.

'Do you still believe in God?' he asked.

'More than ever! And I go to church every Sunday. Not the same church and not just Catholic churches. I pick and choose. I shop around. It's great.'

'What do you do now? I mean, for a living.'

'My job? I'm an information officer at the Lesbian Herstory Archives. How about that? If you're going to come out, you might as well do it in style. People laugh, but actually it's a great place, a great idea – material of every kind, letters, diaries, books, art, movies, every aspect of lesbian life and culture, past and present. You must come visit. We welcome all-comers. Inclusivity is the order of the day. And if you're a lesbian you can donate any three personal items and become part of the Archive's Special Collection. I donated my nun's wimple, my first rosary and a photograph of you and me, Nicholas. It was taken on the Boardwalk when you were about eight. God, he was a lovely child, so pretty. So special. The truth is, he was perfect. We felt he was sort of magic, a kind of enchanted child. I think when he arrived one or two of us, the younger girls, we pretended he was the baby Jesus. Maybe we believed it. Maybe he was.' She put out her hand and let her fingers touch Nick's. She poured out more vodka. 'You know the first time I set eyes on him he was quite naked and *so* beautiful. I thought I'd never seen anything lovelier in all my life. He came to us as a new-born baby and, Lord, the excitement of it! Did you know he arrived at the convent in a straw-filled crib? God save the mark! It was so bitterly cold that night, 6 December, of course, the feast of St Nicholas. That's how we thought of the name. I'm afraid your poor father couldn't be persuaded to tell us your real name, Nicholas, or give us his own for that matter, though Sister Benedict recognised him at once. He was an actor, good-looking. Still is. I saw him on TV only the other day. Some dumb soap, but I recognised him at once – and his name. You'd never forget his name, it's so preposterous. Did you know, Nicholas, your father calls himself Augustus St George? Mary Mother of God, can you believe it?'

It was long after midnight when we got back to our suite at the Chelsea Hotel. There was just one message waiting for us. Dr David Hofmann had called.

Chapter Seven

'A human being, if nothing interfered, would tend to act in such a way at every moment as to try to relieve his strongest tension by gratifying his dearest wish. Every wish that is gratified brings him closer to his goal, which is a feeling of peace and security, or freedom from anxiety.' This was the essential thesis of Dr Berne, the grand old man of West Coast psychiatry when Professor Atkins was one of his students at the University of California Medical School in the 1950s. 'No one ever quite attains the goal, because new wishes are springing up all the time, and there are too many wishes trying for satisfaction at once, so that the mere possibility of gratifying one often increases the tension of the others. Even in sleep there is no peace, and the clattering snorer stirs uneasily at regular intervals through the night.'

Prof Atkins (who claimed to sleep like a baby and protested he never snored) developed his own particular spin on what he called 'the Berne convention'. Accepting that anxiety is an inevitable part of human currency, he maintained 'we should recognize that there are two sides to the coin of anxiety: on the one is apprehension, dread, distress, unease; on the other uncertainty, expectation, anticipation, surprise. If a state of anxiety is a precondition of life itself

("A corpse never gets stage fright, no matter how large his audience"), the wise human should consciously avoid getting hooked on dread, which is the gateway to fear, and actively cultivate an acceptance of surprise, which is one of the keys to the secret garden of happiness.' *Seek Out Surprise! A Self-Help Guide to Living with Anxiety* was the title of the 1962 paperback in which Prof Atkins elaborated on his philosophy and to which Dr Berne contributed a (somewhat equivocal) preface. I must give you a copy one day, Misty. There are some good things in it.

The day after our night out with Sister Peta was certainly packed with surprises, the first of which was that locating the precise whereabouts of Augustus St George that Wednesday morning took less than half an hour. I called Equity and, yes, indeed, Mr St George was a member and would I care for his agent's number? I called the agent and learnt that Nick's father was appearing in the role of the pirate Starkey in the musical *Peter Pan* currently playing at the Philadelphia Opera House. There would be a matinée that afternoon at two-thirty. I should call the theater direct if I wished to reserve seats.

Whether this first surprise of the day eased or heightened Nick's sense of apprehension, I'm not sure. The second surprise, however, appeared to be a distraction without a downside. As we crossed the hotel lobby on our way to catch a cab for Pennsylvania Station we came face to face with Dr Thomas Browne. He greeted us quite casually, as though he had just popped his head around the faculty room door. 'Hi! How are things? New York in the fall – there's nothing like it.' This pleasantry over, he confided that he was on his way to a rendezvous with a Bloody Mary and then vanished into a waiting elevator.

Since this was the mid-semester break, and since the reason we were at the Chelsea was precisely because the school had a special arrangement with the hotel, it was perhaps not so very surprising that we should encounter the headmaster crossing the lobby. That two and half hours later we should come face to face with his deputy crossing a side street in North Philadelphia was, however, a surprise of a different order.

'Yo!' yelled Nick. 'What the hell are you doing here?'

'Doing here?' repeated Mr Rogers. He had the look of a startled ferret: it was not so much alarm at seeing us as the sudden realization that we were seeing him at the very moment when a cruel east wind gusting down North 7th Street was about to wreak havoc and humiliation on the hideous arrangement of his hair. 'Excuse me.' He hustled us into the doorway of a nearby building and, recovering his composure, pinched the moist tip of his nose, briefly inspected his thumb and forefinger, and offered us each a separate wintry smile. 'I might ask the same of you.'

'We're off to the theater,' said Nick with enthusiasm. 'Care to join us?'

'Care to join us? That's most courteous, but I've an appointment here.' He indicated a small plaque just inside the doorway. 'This is a National Historic Landmark. Edgar Allan Poe lived here.'

'I didn't realize that Poe was among your many passions,' said Nick, stepping out into the street to inspect the compact brick building.

'Many passions. You're quite right, Nicholas, he's really more your scene. "All that we see or seem is but a dream within a dream", eh? Poe was an orphan too, you know.' Mr Rogers was now confiding in me.

'Yes, I know, I did a term paper on him once.'

'On him once. Sad story, all that gambling and booze, and the unfortunate child bride. So much genius and dead at forty.'

'The fever called "Living" is conquered at last,' I said.

'Conquered at last.' He licked his lips. 'Yes, well at least young Nicholas is clean-living – so far as we know.' He beamed malevolently at me, and I wondered why, when I had absolutely no cause, I felt so sure he was a thing of evil. 'Take thy beak from out my heart and take thy form from off my door!'

Perhaps he was a mind-reader as well. 'You want me to disappear instanter, so you can get off to your matinée. Quite right. "Keeping time, time, time, in a sort of Runic rhyme." That's why I'm here. There's a clock I've come to inspect, an 1840 Bielefeld. Think, it might have been wound by the hand that wrote "Annabel Lee". Enjoy the show!'

The Philadelphia Opera House is a once-upon-a-time theater. The spangle's all gone now, but once upon a time, my God! It's on Broad Street and Poplar because when Oscar Hammerstein had it built, back in 1907, this was the chic part of town. It's known as 'the Met' because, when Hammerstein sold out, for three sensational seasons the New York Metropolitan Opera Company filled it to capacity. The aim had been to create a palace of culture to rival the revered Academy of Music down the block. The Academy can still lay claim to having the finest acoustics of any auditorium in the world, but for 'the Met', no question, the glory days are past. The stage doorman, looking like an elderly amateur actor playing Mark Twain, reinforced the impression of faded grandeur bordering on decay. He didn't ask who we were or why we wanted to see Mr St George or whether we had an appointment; he simply said, 'Room 22, right to the top, right at the back', and carried on with his crossword.

Although the matinée was only an hour away the theater felt dead, hollow, like a deconsecrated temple. As we climbed the five flights of stone stairs, a trio of desiccated chorus girls clattered past. On the penultimate landing a delicate-looking teenage girl was making heavy weather of ironing a nightshirt. Was it Wendy? If she'd looked up, we might have asked. Nick knocked at the door of Room 22, an odd voice called 'Come!', and we entered.

The room was tiny and spartan and, apparently, empty: bare floorboards, a small window without drapes, a modest dressing table with the traditional square of illuminated mirror above it, two kitchen chairs and a metal clothes-rail on castors, with hangers of costumes crowded at one end and a wooden cage containing an African parrot hanging at the other.

'Oh, God,' I thought, 'he's playing the pirate Starkey as Long John Silver!'

'This is all a bit sad,' said Nick, inspecting the motley collection of sticks of half-used makeup, old wine bottles, photographs, press clippings and unopened mail that lay pell-mell on the dressing table.

Coming to terms with our own disappointments and disillusions is disagreeable, but on the whole we can manage. After all, it's just us. Facing up to those of our children is much more painful; coming face to face with those of our parents can break our hearts.

'All my life I've been dreaming about meeting up with my dad. I've played the scene a thousand times. You name the location, I've set it there – at airports, on railway stations, at the convent, back at Magnolia Hall, in an imaginary farmhouse in the depths of Kansas, with Toto at my heels. I've pictured this reunion *everywhere*—' he laughed – 'except for here. Kirsty, this is pathetic.'

'Bathetic is the word you want! Bathetic – ba – ba, as in bastard!'

An amazing man entered the room. Misty, it was Santa Claus, the real thing, white whiskers, pink cheeks, fur-trimmed red bonnet with tunic to match, shiny black boots and, on his back, a sack full of toys.

Nick stood transfixed. His eyes shone with the light and love I had seen in them that Sunday morning in Charleston. 'Santa Claus.' He said it softly, tenderly, with infinite sweetness.

'Fuck Santa Claus. I'm Augustus St George. Who the hell are you?'

'I'm the guy . . .' said Nick, his voice cracking with laughter and with tears, 'I'm the guy you took to the Convent of the Sacred Heart twenty-eight years ago.'

'Jesus wept!'

Santa dropped his sack, the parrot screeched, and man and boy embraced like father and son.

'My boy, I don't know what to say. How did you find me? *Why* did you find me? It's good to see you, to be sure. Your mother still means a lot to me, God rest her soul.' With one hand he crossed himself; with the other he grasped at the back of the chair. Melodrama was clearly part of his stock-in-trade: the voice, matured in the oak, had begun as a boom and was now hushed to a whisper. 'Oh, my Lord, this is such a surprise, I'm truly overwhelmed. God, I don't even know your name. What do you call yourself?'

'Nick Saint.'

'I like it – snappy. Not much good for the theater, not what we'd call a canopy name, but for the movies it's just right. And this is, er, your fiancée – I trust? She is as welcome as she is beautiful and, boy oh boy, is she beautiful!'

'This is Kirsty Macdonald. She's a friend.'

'Well, I wish I had more friends like her, that's all I can say.' He laughed, a big, hearty laugh, a roast beef of old England laugh, full-blooded, round and rich. This was Santa Claus as Falstaff. 'Kids, this really is most extraordinary. Look, take a seat. Have a drink.'

There was a bottle of French red wine already opened on the dressing table. He splashed some into a mug. 'You'll have to share. I'm not well equipped up here – or well served for that matter.' He paused. 'God, you don't want money, do you? I don't have money. Money is the one thing I have not got. Memories I can give you, old stories, a few laughs, even some unreliable advice – but cash in hand . . . If that's what you're hoping for, Nick – that's the name, isn't it? – then you've climbed the wrong staircase.'

Nick protested that money was the last thing on his mind.

'Good, good, that's a relief. I'm afraid it's the only thing on mine.' He tried out another laugh now, still mellow, but lighter in timbre, higher in pitch, more giggle-and-gurgle than bellow, Pickwick rather than Falstaff. 'As you can imagine, I'd hardly be attired in this ridiculous garb if I wasn't in perpetual want of roll and rhino. The old spondulics. I don't seem to be able to get enough of it, which explains, alas, why I have been obliged to supplement my modest earnings in the theater with forays into what we seasonal Santas call "working the mall". It's only ten dollars an hour, but the joy is nobody recognizes you and you can pick your own hours. I just do mornings. Fuck me. Pardon my French, but if that's the time, I must don my piratical gabardine.' He pulled off his bonnet and his wig, and we made to move. 'No, no, don't go. Just stay put.'

There didn't seem to be room for the three of us if he was going to change. 'We'd like to see the show,' I said.

'You wouldn't, believe me. The original play may be a masterpiece. This musical is a mistake. And my role an insultingly minor one. I don't think you really wish to spend an afternoon huddling in the half-empty stalls with our mid-week matinée crowd, the half-price brigade, the sorriest sampling of simple-minded senior citizenry who, in my view, only come to the Met to get away from Oprah! You just stay put and I'll just come and go. We'll have to turn up the intercom so that we know when I'm required to give what little I'm required to give – but forget the show. It is a show that needs to be forgotten, whereas you two need to be discovered.' (He pronounced it 'discover-red' and, when he'd said it, for a moment let his tongue loll at the corner of his mouth and, catching my eye in his mirror, winked at me. Had Mr Rogers attempted this routine I would have been utterly repelled. Here and now, I was simply charmed.)

Nick was looking at one of the photographs tucked into the side of the dressing-table mirror. 'Who's this? Is this you?'

'Good grief, no. Would that it had been! Sometimes I pretend it's a picture of my father. Don't you know who it is? Look on the back.'

Nick pulled the small picture away from the mirror and turned it over. Pasted on the back was a typed quotation from the *New York Dramatic Mirror*, 1896: 'If ever a man was favored by nature to personate roles of the romantic order – that man is Maurice Barrymore. His face has been likened to that of a Greek god.'

'He's my hero; he was my role model when I was your age, I suppose. I'm thinking of doing him as a one-man show. His life was a mess. His kids were the famous ones, of course, and now there's young Drew, but to me Maurice is the main man. Even before I met your mother he was a kind of icon. He played Orlando right at the start of his career and that was my first Shakespeare too. I did a lot of Shakespeare to begin with. And to acclaim. Yes, I was adored once too.' He brandished his pirate's sabre and raised an eyebrow in my direction. 'I trust you have heard of the Barrymores? Increasingly I find people, kids, even kids in the business, who have no idea who they were.'

Nick was quicker than me. 'Ethel,' he said, 'and John and Lionel.'

'That's my boy! I worked with Lionel once, just a spit and a cough in an episode of *Dr Kildare*. He was the original Dr Gillespie. He had an aura. He had his problems, naturally, it is the badge of all our tribe, but I don't believe he was ever reduced to essaying the role of Santa Claus to help pay for the groceries. Of course, he did play Scrooge on the radio, every Christmas, for twenty years. And he did it in costume, on the radio! When I first heard that, I thought, "That's style!" Now I'm not so sure. A good actor doesn't need a costume, does he? Couldn't I be Santa without dressing up in all this?'

The parrot squawked. Augustus St George pulled on

the striped shirt of the stage pirate. 'Is there anything more pitiable than a jealous parakeet? He is so accustomed to commanding my exclusive attention that he can't cope with the competition. I was horrified to learn the other day that parrots can live just as long as we do. I've had him only eight years. Can you imagine? I'll have him squawking at my death-bed: "That's all there is. There isn't any more."' He fastened his sword, adjusted his black eyepatch and donned his pirate's hat. The transformation was complete. 'I must go. My public awaits. I shall not be long. My public gets ridiculously little of me in this lousy production.' He moved the wine bottle off some papers and handed the top sheet to Nick. 'Help yourself to more wine. And if you're interested in Maurice, read that. I've only just come across it. His kids thought he was mad, you know. Had him locked up. It's a risky business this. *A bientôt.*'

Nick watched him go with wonder and amusement. 'What do you make of him?' he asked.

'I think he's great. Amazing.'

'Do I look like him?'

'No,' I smiled. 'You look like Maurice, the Greek god.' Nick looked at the sheet of paper Augustus had handed to him:

> John Barrymore, art student, nineteen years old, residing at No 61 West Thirty-sixth Street, being duly sworn deposes and says that on the 29th day of March 1901, in the city of New York, county of New York, Maurice Barrymore, now in Bellevue Hospital, was acting in a strange manner, to wit: talking in an incoherent manner and in danger of doing bodily harm to himself and the members of his family.

> Deponent verily believes that the said Maurice Barrymore is disordered in his senses and unfit to be at large, and prays that he may be committed to the care and charge of the Commissioner of Public Charities for examination as to his sanity.

Between the shows, the old actor allowed us to entertain him to supper at 'one of his clubs', the Franklin on Mt Vernon Street, 'a gentleman's establishment of the old school'. 'The joy of provincial life is that they take all this pretentious nonsense seriously. My clubs in New York cost twice as much, but they don't do it half as well. You must have the beef off the trolley, my dear, pink and tender, cut slantingly to the bone. And, Nick, while my cuffs are frayed, my nose is sound and a Nuits St Georges would be much appreciated. The actor playing Hook only drinks spirits. It shows in his performance. Sir James Barrie wrote plays for actors who drank claret and Burgundy. Oh, Lord, this wine is good. Another glass or two of this and I'll be ready to revive my Othello.'

He was a handsome man, about sixty, I supposed, inevitably (given his enthusiasm for the savory and his delight in the dessert wine) a little over-florid and thickset, and I imagine the silver head of hair was probably thinner than he would have liked it to be. He made his chief impression with his voice: it was what gave him his special presence, his particular style, his touch of magic. His conversation revolved entirely around the theater, actors and acting. I asked him what gave an actor charisma.

'You mean star quality? You're sitting there wondering why I've almost got it, but not quite. I've been wondering the same thing for nigh on half a century! I don't know about the movies, but on stage I recognize the attributes of a star player when I see them. There's authority, for a start. And energy; concentrated energy always, and boundless vitality as required. Clarity. Certainty of execution. An athletic voice. I score with the vocal *chiaroscuro*, you'll have noticed. Style. A peculiar grace. Eyes count for a lot. The look is always important, but not looks, of course. They're just a bonus. Originality of temperament, call it idiosyncracy. Hell, on a good night I can muster most of that, but then there's that little bit extra, that mystery ingredient, the sprinkling of woofle dust. I simply don't have it. The Barrymores, lucky bastards, had it by the bucketful. It's the one thing that's holding me back from doing the one-man show. Can you play a star when you're not a star? The answer must be no.'

Quite suddenly he turned towards Nick, who was sitting on the banquette beside him. 'You do realize that Maurice Barrymore is your great-great-grandfather? You did know that, didn't you?'

Nick, who until that afternoon had not even heard of the senior Barrymore, did not know what to say. He had been biding his time, waiting to ask about his mother. Perhaps the moment had come. 'I don't even know . . .'

'No, no, you're quite right. It's wrong of me to assert such a thing. So much about Barrymore is shrouded in mystery. For a start, that wasn't his real name. He invented it. He had to. No birth certificate. Poor fellow, didn't even know when he was born. All I can tell you, Nick my boy, is that your mother believed her father was the grandson of Maurice Barrymore. Of course, the old boy played the field. As well as the fabulous Georgie Drew, the mother of the famous three, he had a second wife and countless mistresses, several notorious, some celebrated, a few simply sweethearts he encountered on the road. According to Charlotte, your mother, one of these young beauties – all Maurice's women were impossibly beautiful! – was a tall, dark Polish princess – well, not exactly a princess, but she too was a love child and the story was that her father had been a Polish prince – and this heavenly creature, Helena Bednarczyk – not a canopy name to be sure – famous though for her piercing eyes and blue-black tresses, managed to win an extra special place in our hero's heart not only because of her extraordinary allure but also, and this is the point, because she was a sensational Rosalind. The fruit of their union was a girl called Celia, and Celia, as I remember it, was Charlotte's father's mother!' He sat back, triumphant, and sipped his wine. 'All those women; no wonder the poor bastard went mad.'

'And my mother?'

'She was a Barrymore, *sans doute*. If anyone had star quality, Charlotte Richards had it. To her fingertips. When she came on, wham, all eyes came straight to her. And stayed with her. It wasn't just presence and instinct. She had impeccable technique. With one turn of the head she could take in every part of the house. She wasn't flashy, she wasn't showy, she just knew what she was doing, and had a certain quality that's all too rare. I suppose these days we'd say she was properly "centered". She could take a great barn of a place like the Met and turn it into an intimate studio. From the word go, she had you in the palm of her hand. Of course, she was sensationally beautiful, as you know—'

'I don't know,' said Nick. 'I didn't know her name until just now.'

A flicker of disbelief, a tremor of suspicion, showed

on the old actor's face. He tilted his head and looked at Nick with narrowed eyes. 'Is't possible?' he murmured, then grunted as if to acknowledge that, yes, Nick might be telling the truth, and immediately felt inside his coat pocket for his wallet. He flicked it open and pulled out a wadge of folded bills, credit cards, receipts, visiting cards, square inches of yellowing newsprint. Expertly, like a close-up magician, with just one hand he riffled through them (with the other he gently swirled his wine) and finally, now with his quizzical expression evaporating into a satisfied and kindly smile, conjured up a small photograph, no more than passport size, and handed it to Nick.

'The fringed curtains of thine eyes advance, and say what thou seest yond.'

'It's in color,' said Nick.

'What did you expect? Sepia? I'm not that old.'

'Is that you?'

'Yes, but the point, young man, is the young lady. Isn't she gorgeous? That's your mother.'

Nick held the tiny photograph close to his eyes, and smiled. He passed it over to me. The girl was certainly good looking, fair, wide-eyed, slender, her blonde hair in a sort of Beatles bob. She looked a long way away and she was dressed as a boy.

'How did you meet?'

'Summer stock. In Maine. My first and last experience of open air theater. The repertoire was predictable, even if the weather was not. Wilder, Miller, Shakespeare. Charlie was just starting out, but she had the three juvenile leads and walked away with every show. Everyone fell for her. At once. Wham bam! Offstage or on, you couldn't resist our Charlie. It wasn't just her looks or her talent. She had a sweetness I can't express. It sounds corny, but she was just so nice.'

Nick said nothing. 'Did you love her very much?' I asked.

'I adored her. We all did. The whole gang. It was a magic summer, with a magic girl at the center of it. She sort of mesmerized us. We danced around her maypole. And, of course, we wanted to make it last. Nothing lasts, but we didn't know that then. She was a year or so younger than the rest of us, but we were all kids really and we wanted it to go on for ever and ever. I suppose we didn't want to grow up. There's a play in it somewhere, isn't there? We were the Lost Boys, and Charlie was our Wendy. That's why when we got back to New York we decided we'd share an apartment – not just for the rest of the year, but for ever. I can hear her saying it, "for ever and ever, Amen."'

He held his wine glass under his nose and sighed gently. 'And for a year or more it worked. It worked great. Charlie was on the edge of stardom. She was going to be very big, we all knew that. Her agent wanted her to move out to LA, but she wouldn't. She loved the theater. And she loved Chelsea.'

I glanced at Nick. He was already looking at me.

'We had an apartment on West 20th. I'm still there.'

'Were you married?'

'Good God, no.'

'Didn't you want to marry her? Didn't she want to marry you?'

'I'm not the marrying kind. She knew that.'

'But you slept with her.'

'Never. No. No, it was never like that. Good God, Nick, I'm not your father. You didn't think that, did you? I'm not anybody's father. Of that I am entirely certain.'

The waiter refilled our glasses. 'It's gone seven, Mr St George.'

Chapter Eight

We walked back to the theater with Augustus St George, arm in arm (his in mine, mine in Nick's), and kept him company in his dressing room until the intermission. Nick had been so ready, so eager, to embrace the old actor as his father, had committed himself at once and so completely, that the sudden reversal quite winded him. He was drained, and it showed. Augustus, by contrast, was exhilarated.

'*Quel* mix-up! If, inadvertently, I appear to have accepted your hospitality, your more than generous hospitality, under false pretences, I apologize. *Ce n'est pas le vrai papa!* It really is the stuff of a French farce. Or a Greek tragedy.' On went the eyepatch. 'A different eye tonight. I am hoping to throw Captain Hook. I played Oedipus once, you know. At college, way before I knew your mother, you'll be relieved to hear – though, come to think of it, in maturity she'd have been the definitive Jocasta.' He let slip a high-pitched laugh (Jack Nicholson as The Joker) which rapidly subsided into a low, bubbling, chortle (Jim Backus as Mr Magoo). 'I never understood what the fuss was about. Oedipus had no idea that the guy he was killing was his father. It was a simple case of mistaken identity. So what? Big deal.'

Whether or not he had seemed a credible parent, he

now looked an improbable pirate, preposterous, in fact. He steadied himself with an avuncular hand on Nick's shoulder and then moved with an elaborate swagger towards the door.

Nick looked after him. 'Who was my father?'

'Ah, now you're asking . . .'

'I need to know. Please.'

'Do you? Really and truly? While I descend and strut my stuff you may care to ponder on it. Isn't it enough to have uncovered your mother – and to have learnt that she was one of the loveliest creatures who ever trod God's earth? Do you need more?'

Nick needed more. I knew that.

Misty, I trust you love your parents, but I hope you don't feel the need to brood about the nature of your relationship with them. I loved my parents too; I love them still, but, in the best sense, I took them quite for granted, always. You will say it was only because they were there that I could, and you will be right. I suppose I had Professor Atkins too, as a kind of surrogate father, but that was his choice not mine, his problem not mine. I welcomed his love, but I knew it was conditional and full of complexities. My own mom and dad I loved much more simply. I needed them, naturally, but over time I came to realize that I needed them just to be, not to do. For me the fact of their existence was enough. I shall be grateful all my days for the uncomplicated, undemanding, unerring certainty of their love. It's there like the sun, brilliant and warm and never-failing. When I moved East I didn't call them much, or write: I didn't feel the need and I knew they didn't feel the want. My only fear for them was lest they lose one another. When I had been in my teens and realized for the first time that not only did they love one another but they were in love, powerfully, passionately, forever caught in the heady throes of a magnificent lifelong affair, I found the idea embarrassing, disgusting even. Now it moved me and made me hope that a benevolent God, or a kind murderer, would eventually take them together.

Until he knew who they were, Nick couldn't take his parents for granted. I understood that. Perhaps Augustus St George understood it too, because when he returned at the intermission he said at once, 'We must meet up in New York. I have pictures of your mother. I may even have some footage of her and the gang. Home movies from the swinging sixties. I've several of her letters for sure and a few reviews that'll gladden your heart. Your mom's career was brief, but, boy, was it sweet. She was a Barrymore all right: she never got a bad notice.'

'And my father? Who was my father?'

'Well, now, that's more difficult.' He hesitated, but purely for effect. 'To be frank, there could be several candidates.' Nick didn't react. He sensed the old ham was playing a game. '*Mon dieu*, doesn't that sound ungallant? Certainly I've got no proof, but you've got to remember it was the age of Aquarius, flower power and free love, and Charlie Richards was without doubt the loveliest girl in town.'

'I want to know. If you can help, I would be so grateful.'

Augustus St George sank down on his chair, flicked up his eyepatch and looked at Nick in the mirror. 'I never liked him much.'

'You do know who he was, then?'

'Yes, my boy, I suppose I do. I never liked him much and

I never trusted him. That's why I took you to the Convent of the Sacred Heart. I told him you'd be safe, but I didn't tell him where I was taking you. He couldn't acknowledge you. I realized that. I accepted that. He wouldn't follow you. I knew that too. And even if he did, I reckoned Coney Island would be the last place he'd look. You'd be safe there. Always.'

The intercom crackled into life. 'Act Two beginners, please.' The parrot squawked.

Nick asked, 'What was his name?'

The unlikely gentleman pirate peered bleakly at the half-inch of red wine at the bottom of his mug and breathed out through his nose, slowly, heavily. He got to his feet. 'Sebastian. He was called Sebastian. It's a lovely name.'

'Is he still alive?'

'Oh yes, alive – and well – and *still* younger than me, dammit. I have not spoken to him since that night, whenever it was, almost thirty years ago now, but I see him in the distance from time to time. I see him and I wonder . . .'

'Will you introduce me to him?'

Augustus St George moved towards the door. The old trouper was getting ready to make his exit. 'No, that I won't do. I won't speak to him ever again. And I'm not sure you'd be wise to either, my boy.' He began to open the door, building the drama. 'I won't introduce you to him, but I'll show him to you if you want.'

'When?' Nick was full of hope, and trepidation.

'Tomorrow, if you like. I'll come up to New York for the day.'

The intercom spluttered again. 'Mr St George to the stage, please. Act Two is about to begin.'

'What about your morning as Santa?' I asked.

'Fuck Santa.' I must say he said it with great style. 'I loathe the idea of Christmas starting in October. Christmas before Thanksgiving is obscene. I shall call in and tell them that Santa is sick. The truth is they're the sick ones, but I shan't tell them that because on Friday I'll be grateful for the forty dollars. You have given me a quite extraordinary day today. Tomorrow, if that's what you want, I'll do my best to repay the compliment. I'll be at the Chelsea by noon. *A demain, mes enfants.*'

It was a little after midnight when we arrived back at the hotel. Standing at the edge of the deserted lobby, waiting for the elevator, we could hear Dr Browne in the bar. The surprises of the day were not quite behind us. Mr Rogers was with him. In stage whispers, rhyme and song, they were enunciating clearly and loudly in the time-honored fashion of the hopelessly drunk. '"It was the night before Christmas and all through the house—"'

'"It was night in the lonesome October of my most immemorial year." Have you read *The Murders in the Rue Morgue*? I bought a copy this afternoon.'

'OJ is innocent, OK?'

Mr Rogers snickered through a sneeze. 'That's another good reason for not recruiting him. Where did I read that a third of all murderers genuinely believe in their own innocence. Nietzsche explained it.'

'Nietzsche explained everything.'

'"My memory says I did it. My self-regard says I did not. My memory gives way."'

'Nietzsche's time has not yet come. He was born posthumously.'

'That's very good. Who said, "To endure is all"?'

'Who cares?'

'I do—'

'And I do, 'cos all I want is you!'

The elevator came. I asked Nick, 'Were they always like this?'

'No, it's gotten much worse. Something's wrong, but I don't know what it is.'

Augustus St George looked much older in the morning. Overnight, and dramatically, he seemed to have shrunk, his face had sagged, his eyes had dimmed and turned from azure to milky gray. His hair was disheveled and appeared to have thinned still further. Even his bravura baritone was transmuted to a reedy whistle.

'I know what you're thinking. Yesterday a fortress, today a ruin. It's just a trick of the light. It's probably got something to do with age, and energy too, and giving altogether too many performances mid-week. Anyroad, I made it. Let's take a cab.'

We drove first around the block, no more than a few hundred yards, to the corner of 22nd and 10th Avenue. He made us wait in the cab while he struggled out and went up the steps and disappeared into the darkened porch of what looked like a miniature Romanesque church miraculously transported to the Middle West Side from the plains of Lombardy. He returned almost at once, breathless, but noticeably invigorated. 'Come, Watson, the game's afoot! We're going to the Cathedral Church of St John the Divine. Have you been before? I think you'll like it. It's amazing.'

It *is* amazing, Misty, and if you've not been you must go someday. There's no need to rush. It isn't finished yet, and they say it won't be till around 2050. A clergyman named

Horatio Potter dreamed it up in the 1870s: he wanted to create the biggest church in America. Even half-complete, it has to be the biggest Gothic cathedral in the world: you could fit Notre-Dame and Canterbury inside it all at once and still have room for the Wee Kirk in the Heather. It is monumental: 600 feet long, 146 feet wide, 177 feet high (when finally they reach their peak the cloud-capped towers will top 290 feet); the forty-foot rose window is made from more than ten thousand pieces of glass; the great west front doors (cast in the foundry that gave us the Statue of Liberty) stand eighteen feet high and weigh three tons. Ten thousand worshippers can congregate here together. It is handsome: the epic façade does take your breath away; from the apex of the roof Gabriel trumpets its glory. It is full of objects of real beauty, ancient and modern: a magnificent pulpit hewn from Tennessee marble; the Berberini tapestries from the seventeenth century; portals fabulously carved from Burmese teakwood; the Menorah lights descended from the Temple of Solomon; the golden chests in the chapel of St Saviour, a gift from the king of Siam. It is fully worthy of its place in the *Guinness Book of World Records* and the *Smithsonian Guide to Historic America*, but I have to confess that while I was gobsmacked by its awesome grandeur I didn't begin to feel its soul. It was like arriving at a gargantuan medieval airport, something Michael Eisner might have conceived had he been born and bred in thirteenth-century France.

As we crossed the nave and looked up towards the rafters, Nick, who had been before and knew the form, went 'Wow!', and instantly won over the bright-eyed young guide who now latched onto us with the flattering assumption that we too were on our way to the Chapel of the Arts for the regular Thursday lunchtime poetry reading.

'Alas,' said Augustus, who appeared to be gaining in vigor by the minute, 'not this week. Appearances are so deceptive. We may look as if we're in the poetry line, but in truth we're here to celebrate the Feast of St Isidore the Farm Servant. I understand there's an ecumenical service of some kind. Does that sound right?'

'It sure does, but it began at twelve. It's in the Chapel of the Labors of Mankind. I'll show you. He sounds a neat guy, Isidore. Tilled the same field for sixty years. Spain or somewhere.'

As we followed the young man, I noticed the way Nick was watching him, closely, with amusement and affection. Was he simply charmed or was there something predatory in the look?

We passed the Chapel of the Arts, where they were setting out the chairs in Poets' Corner. Our guide paused and pointed to the inscriptions on the floor: with each remembered writer a legend meant to signify. 'Thy will be done in art as it is in heaven' for Willa Cather; 'Live all you can; it's a mistake not to' for Henry James. Nick touched my arm and smiled as he pointed to Edgar Allan Poe: 'Out of space; out of time'. I looked about and was quite surprised to find Mr Rogers wasn't there.

As we approached the Chapel of the Labors of Mankind, Augustus held us back and ceremoniously dismissed our guide with an elaborately mouthed, but silent, 'Thank you so much.' The boy brought his hands together as if for prayer, tilted his head and bowed towards us like a blushing geisha. As, coyly, he retreated, his eyes caught Nick's and one of them said, or perhaps it was both, 'God bless!'

Lying in bed that night I tried to work out why this

brief incident had so impressed itself upon me. It was, I realized eventually, because I had seen that exact look once before. Years ago, I had been on a Greyhound bus traveling from San Francisco to LA and for some reason, I can't remember what it was or where it was, we had to make an unscheduled stop at a gas station. I didn't get off the bus, but out of the window I saw a boy I thought I recognized. In fact, I didn't know him at all, but he stared at me for a second or so and then he smiled, a wonderful blinding smile, and I smiled back and, suddenly, and for just a moment in time, we were in love, completely and utterly in love, and – this I firmly believe – even as the bus drove off we both of us knew it. It occurred to me that night that what that boy at the gas station did for me, just the once and now so long ago, Nick was capable of doing to almost anyone almost all the time! Nick could fall in love with you – and you could fall in love with him – instantly, immediately and completely. It wasn't profound, it wasn't complicated, it didn't lead anywhere, but it was love all the same, instant, pure and simple.

In the Chapel of the Labors of Mankind, standing before the altar were two priests: one, the Protestant, middle-aged, round, smooth, inscrutable (had we found him in Poets' Corner we'd have cast him as Wallace Stevens); the other, the Catholic, older, taller, grander, craggy visage, shaggy locks, snowy white hair, and bearded (Walt Whitman, no question). He delivered the blessing like an Old Testament prophet: 'May the God who binds up the broken-hearted, who proclaims freedom to those held captive by poverty, and promises justice to all who mourn its loss, bless you with beauty instead of ashes, the oil of gladness in place of grief, and instead of your spirit of despair, a garment of unending praise; through Jesus Christ our Lord, Amen.'

Nick echoed the amen.

'That's him,' whispered Augustus St George. 'That's Father Sebastian.'

'I think,' he said, lifting the glass of Chardonnay and holding it up to the light to inspect it, 'I think he may have killed her.'

'Who?'

'Sebastian.'

'Killed who?'

'Your mother. I think Sebastian may have murdered your mother.'

We were downstairs in the Poplar Tavern, in a corner at the back. Augustus, his force restored, had led us there, brooking no argument. It was a familiar haunt of his, he explained, 'from way back – when I was on the fringes of the Beat generation – yes, that long ago', only a couple of blocks from the cathedral and always full of bright young things. 'The waiters are all students, so are the customers. It's good to be surrounded by the young now and again. We'll get ourselves a bottle of wine and I'll tell you everything I know.'

'I don't believe what I'm hearing,' said Nick.

'You don't have to,' said Augustus, taking a gulp of the wine. 'I have no proof, not a shred. I have no *reason* for what I'm saying, just a feeling, an instinct. On the night Charlie died, Sebastian told me she had taken her own life. That was a lie. I couldn't prove it to you, but I knew it as soon as he said it, sensed it. Smelt it. Something rotten in the state of Denmark.'

Nick looked warily at the older man, remembering how completely he had accepted him as a father only twenty-four hours before. Was he just an old fraud, a spinner of yarns, a teller of tales? Nick thought of Theo Quincy. He invented adventures for himself all the time, sometimes to annoy, sometimes to impress, often just for the sake of it. He once told Nick that he had tried to poison his younger brother by spiking his milkshakes with rat poison. He told the story at length, elaborately, with graphic detail, came back to it again and again over most of a semester, and then one night, quite suddenly, declared that not a single word of the sinister saga had been true. He had never even had a younger brother. Had Augustus St George even known Nick's mother?

'How did my mother die?' he asked.

'I don't know,' said Augustus. 'All I know is that I got in from rehearsal around seven and, as I came into the apartment, the telephone was ringing. It was Sebastian. He was troubled, but in control. He wanted me to come round to the church right away. He said, "Something terrible's happened. Charlie's dead." When I got to the church, he let me in round the back, through the vestry.'

'Was he a priest then?' I asked the question. Nick was gazing intently at our guest, wondering what – and whether – to believe.

'Just. He had started out as an actor. And he'd been good, but not good enough. He had a superfluity of ambition, but an insufficiency of talent. It's a common problem among aspiring thespians. Sebastian was consumed with ambition. He admitted it. He seemed to revel in it. "I am going to make my mark on the world!" he'd say. And we'd say, "How?" And he'd say, "I don't yet know, but there's a still small voice inside me telling me that I am destined to join the ranks of the great immortals. Mock me if you must, but I'll have the last laugh." I'd always mistrusted him; his arrogance was risible; his manner insufferably self-conscious. But Charlie, she fell for him right away. It was love at first sight – wham, bam, the whole caboodle.' He sipped his wine, 'Ah, yes, I remember it well. The first day of rehearsals, 6 January '64, Twelfth Night. That wasn't the show. The show was *Romeo and Juliet.* Charlie was Juliet. Charlie was perfection. I was Mercutio, not bad, and Sebastian was Tybalt. Tybalt! Christ almighty, Charlotte Richards was the truest, sweetest, surest Juliet of her generation, and she fell for the smartass playing Tybalt! It is unheard of. In the history of world theater, no Juliet has ever fallen for Tybalt. It shouldn't happen, it shouldn't be allowed to happen. As far as I'm concerned it doesn't happen. But it did. He was good looking, I suppose, and he had the gift of the gab. God, how he talked. He never stopped. The words spewed out of him in a relentless torrent. And he didn't just say it all. He knew it all.' Augustus paused to take another sip of wine and to smile – at himself, at us, at the nostalgic recollection? It was hard to tell.

'I viewed Sebastian as something of a fool. And a phony. Maybe I was wrong. I was alone, that's for sure. The rest of the company liked him; the young ones were awed, the older ones amused, and Charlie, well, she simply adored him. He swept her off her feet. She'd never been in love before. She was only eighteen and this appeared to be her first encounter with a professional charmer. Off stage, Sebastian could dazzle, and he did. On stage, nothing much happened, and he knew it. We poor players, good or bad, we want to be loved. In performance, if we know what we're doing, we can command that love, control it, even. As an actor Sebastian was okay, never less than competent, sometimes quite stylish, but it was chocolate-box stuff, showy, shallow, fundamentally uninteresting. In the green room, out at a bar, it was different. He had a kind of star quality then; you noticed him come into the room, and when he left, the place felt emptier. He was a great seducer – not literally, but emotionally. I reckon that's why he gave up theater and went into the church. He said he'd found his true vocation. I doubt it. He knew he'd never be a star on stage, but he was keenly aware of his own strengths, his own power, and to be a star in the spiritual firmament might well be within his capabilities. As a performer, particularly as an interpreter of other men's lines, he wasn't that special. As a preacher, using his own personality, it might be different. As a priest, with the power of the confessional at his disposal, he'd be in his element.'

It was my turn to smile now. 'You really don't like him, do you?'

'I didn't dislike him then. I didn't believe him, that was all. I could see what he was up to, and it wasn't to my taste. Charlie, poor child, believed him and believed in him, absolutely. He had the sort of power over her that she had over an audience. She was transfixed by him. Within a month of that first day she said to me, "I know you don't understand, but he's my man. I love him, I'm going to marry him, I'm going to have his children." She was like Alice falling down the rabbit hole, falling ever more hopelessly in love as she tumbled, down and down, deeper and deeper. And when she got to the bottom it was a crash-landing. Once he'd hooked her, he told her of his so-called vocation. Then she was trapped. The way forward was blocked. And she was too far gone to be able to find the way back. Of course, that was another reason for opting for the priesthood. He could protect himself, go as far as he wanted with the perfect excuse for going no further.'

Nick listened and said nothing. 'Why do you think he killed her?' I asked. 'To protect himself, to safeguard his reputation, his career?'

'It was more than that. He wanted to get rid of her. She had become oppressive. Off and on they went out together for five years. There were months when they wouldn't meet; he was at the seminary, she was on tour; she dated other guys; she had a great capacity for love; but Sebastian was her man. He was her obsession. Give him his due, he loved her too, in his fashion. But he loved himself more, much more. It's a common enough story. And then, when she fell pregnant, the crisis was upon them both. She may have been an actress, she may have been a Barrymore, but deep down Charlie Richards was just another home-town girl. She wanted a ring on her finger, a husband on her arm, a white picket fence out front, the American dream. A nightmare for Sebastian. Something had to give or something had to be done. She wouldn't give, she wouldn't give up, she wouldn't go away. I doubt that what he did was premeditated. I don't think even he could have murdered a pregnant woman, and he was far too conscious of his own worth, far too vain, to do damage to his own flesh and blood, but the moment the child was safely delivered he saw his chance to free himself, and to free her. He knew she was trapped. She knew it. Now that her baby was born, he could release her, let her go. It was a mercy killing.'

At last Nick spoke. 'Did he tell you all this?'

'Christ, no. It's my wild surmise. When I got to the church he was amazingly cool, almost serene. He told me that he'd gone to her apartment – she had a room in the Flower District, she'd moved out of our place about six months before – and found her there, virtually unconscious, lying dying on her bed, an empty bottle of morphine at her side, the newborn baby in her arms. He gave her the last rites and promised to find her son a good home. He said she died minutes after he arrived. He didn't know what to do. He said he panicked. He heard a noise on the stairs. He took the baby, wrapped it up in whatever he could find, and climbed out the back window and down the fire escape. He brought the baby with him to the church and called me. I asked him where the baby was now and he said he'd hidden him in the church, in the chapel where they set out the nativity scene. He led me from the vestry along a candle-lit aisle towards a huge effigy of an angel. I remember it had great golden wings outstretched. As we approached I could hear the baby whimpering. I looked down at the tiny figure lying in the crib. It was like the old gag where the Three Wise Men pitch up at the stable and one of them trips and says, "Jesus!" and Joseph looks up and says, "That's a neat name for a boy." I saw the child wrapped in a towel, lying in the manger, and when I whispered, "Christ Almighty!" Sebastian knelt down and touched the baby's face and said, "No. Nicholas. My little St Nicholas." What do you do with a man like that?'

Chapter Nine

Augustus St George drained his glass, smacked his lips, checked his watch and slapped his hands down firmly on the table. 'I must catch my train. I fear all I've done is bring confusion to your lives. Please accept my apologies.'

'There's nothing to apologize for,' said Nick. 'I needed to know.'

'Maybe. At least now, when you screw up, you've got parents to blame.' He produced a fresh wheezy chuckle from his extensive repertoire (Frank Morgan in *The Wizard of Oz*) and pushed his chair back from the table. 'The first time I came here,' he said, 'Jack Kerouac was sitting there, just there, by the coat-rack. He was correcting proofs of *Lonesome Traveler*.'

Was it true? Had Kerouac ever been to the Poplar Tavern? Had Augustus seen him there? Was this just another fantasy and, if it was, did it matter? I remembered Dr Browne telling me how he and his colleagues reinvented great swaths of their lives, exaggerated actual experiences, heightened them, modified them, improved on them, denied them altogether, not for any sinister or malevolent reason, but to make themselves seem more interesting, more interesting to the world and more interesting to themselves.

'Over time,' said Dr Browne, 'I've turned into a caricature of the character I have imagined myself to be. I have conjured up a past for myself that may or may not be strictly verifiable, but I've told the tale so often that now I've lost track of what did or didn't happen. If we're living the lie, and living it to the full, who's to say what's true or false?'

It seemed different with Augustus. The old actor didn't produce his lines so much for the effect upon himself as to please his audience. He wasn't showing off for his own sake. He was a performer who wanted to give his audience what he sensed they wanted. Nick had come to him wanting parents. Parents had been provided.

In the cab going to Penn Station, none of us said much. Nick gazed out the window, listless and distant; Augustus held my hand. He looked weary once more. The energy that he had summoned up in the cathedral, the sparkle he had evinced over lunch, had ebbed and faded. He knew what I was thinking. 'In younger and happier days I did not value my body as I might have done and the price I pay is that it is no longer entirely mine to command. Curiously, I could still do the opening scenes of *Lear*, the big stuff, the bully-boy, the lion on the roar, but the decline into madness and the end, when he's broken and moonstruck and oh-so-gentle, that's beyond me now. It's the subtle moments that really require the energy.' Another laugh. 'Bah! Humbug!'

The cab jerked into 33rd Street. '*Eh bien, mes enfants.* Remember, it is but a tale told by an idiot, and I'm not going to let you make me feel too guilty. You sought me out. You asked for it.'

'Yes,' said Nick, 'I'm grateful, truly. There's a lot to think about, that's all.'

'I know, kid. And I never got to show you the home movies. Edited highlights of Charlie's Viola. You'll be impressed.' He turned back to me as he clambered out of the car. 'I think, my dear, you'll find the fragment of my Orsino quite dashing. If bullshit be the food of love indeed! Thank you for lunch. Thank you for last night. Sebastian played Fabian, natch. A performance that has not been immortalized on celluloid. Thank God.' He leant back into the cab and leaned across me to squeeze Nick on the arm. '*Au revoir, mon brave*. Let's meet up after Christmas. You've got my number.'

'I'm not sure where I'll be after Christmas,' said Nick.

If Augustus heard, he didn't take it in, or, if he did, he decided not to let it delay him. He simply waved a cheery wave and banged the roof of the cab. '*A la prochaine fois*. Take care now!'

'The Chelsea Hotel, please,' said Nick, smiling his shy, self-conscious, little-boy-lost smile at me.

'What was all that about not knowing where you'll be after Christmas?'

'I can't go on like this, Kirsty. Something's got to give. I'm setting myself a deadline and, under the circumstances, Christmas seems appropriate. What do you say? Don't answer.' He laughed. 'I shouldn't have got you involved in all this.'

'Why did you? Why me?'

'I thought it was destiny. I'm a fool.'

'I'm the fool,' I thought. 'I thought it was love.'

'Do you think the son of a murderer is more or less likely to be a murderer himself?'

Through the grille I stared at the thick, ugly neck of the cab-driver. Because of that neck, and probably because he was a cab-driver too, I took it for granted that the poor man was brutish and ignorant. I had no evidence. I was simply making assumptions. We all assume so much so much of the time.

We were in West 23rd Street now, drawing up at the hotel. Abruptly Nick lurched forward and yelled, 'Drive on. *Drive on!* Keep going. Don't stop.' As the car jerked away from the kerb I looked back and saw, standing close together on the sidewalk, Mr Rogers and Father Sebastian. They were talking animatedly, comfortably, and shaking hands. It was an exaggerated handshake, prolonged, unreal, overdemonstrative, sustained as though for the cameras.

'What's going on?'

'That's what I'd like to know.'

The thick neck twisted back towards us. Despite the glint of gold around the mouth, there was no menace in the voice at all. 'Where the hell do you want to go now?'

'I don't know,' said Nick. 'I don't know where I've come from. I don't know who I am. I don't know where I'm going.'

'So long as you know which of you is paying, I don't give a damn. I'll just keep driving round the block.'

Nick clapped his hands. 'Let's go to the movies.'

'Okay,' I said. 'Maybe *Miracle on 34th Street* is showing someplace.'

'You bitch!' He began to laugh. 'I deserved that.' It was his easy, self-mocking laugh. 'You are absolutely right, little Miss Mac. I am a self-indulgent, self-absorbed, self-regarding fool. And a lousy traveling companion. You did not come to New York to go to the movies.

We must see the sights. Brooklyn Bridge. Rockefeller Plaza. Do you skate? Or are you more in the mood for culture? We shall go to the museums! Given that we are staying at the Chelsea, I think it's appropriate that I take you to see the Warhols at the Whitney. Don't you?' Suddenly he seemed so happy. 'I take it you've not been before?'

I would have remembered, Misty. The Whitney Museum of American Art, on Madison at 75th, is located in one of the ugliest award-winning buildings I know. It is a brute of a structure, massive, forbidding, top-heavy, windowless, heartless, graceless. It has a granite façade, but no grandeur; it speaks of power, but without passion. You feel that if he had still been around when it was built, Stalin would have approved.

As we crossed the sidewalk and climbed the museum steps, Nick's face was alight once more. I was pleased, but puzzled. 'Do you like this kind of building?' I asked.

'No, I *hate* it. You know I have this theory that something went awry in the late sixties? Well, this could be a part of it. The building's a monster, that's for sure. But you'll like some of what you see inside.'

I didn't like what I saw first. It was entitled 'The Wait' and depicted an old woman (represented by a sheep's skull in a bottle), surrounded by yellowing photographs and faded memorabilia, and surmounted by a caged and mangy bird that croaked and cawed bleakly like Mr Rogers' raven. 'This is gross.'

'Don't be distracted,' said Nick. 'We know what we've come for. We're looking for Mr Warhol.'

We found him. He wasn't looking his best. He was sitting on a sofa, upright, half-naked, dead behind the eyes. The portrait was undeniably striking, but the image was pitiable. He looked so old, so worn, so sick.

'The icon of his age,' said Nick.

'A far cry from Santa.'

I didn't look towards Nick, but I felt him smile. 'About as far as you can get.'

'First Valerie shot him, then Alice painted him. I knew them both.' I recognized the voice at once. It was Miss Haversham. She was standing at our side, gazing intently at the picture. She didn't pause to greet us or marvel at the coincidence of finding herself with two of her colleagues in such an unexpected spot. She took a small step closer and, with her head, gestured towards the painting. 'You see the scars, the bandages. Not all murder is in the mind. Valerie Solanis tried to kill him. Quite literally. She failed, of course. She was a failure. So many of them were. It was the week after Edie took her fatal overdose. They'd both had their fifteen minutes of fame. Valerie was one of the founders of SCUM.'

I looked towards her.

'The Society for Cutting Up Men,' she explained with a certain thin-lipped relish. 'The murder attempt was part of her mission. Read the sign.'

To the left of the portrait was a printed notice about the picture. It included an extract from Valerie Solanis's SCUM Manifesto:

> Life in this society being, at best, an utter bore and no aspect of society being at all relevant to women, there remains to civic-minded, responsible, thrill-seeking females only to overthrow the government, eliminate the money system, institute complete automation, and destroy the male sex. SCUM will kill all men

> who are not in the Men's Auxiliary of SCUM. Men in the Men's Auxiliary are those men who are working diligently to eliminate themselves.

'She had a sense of humor,' I said.

Miss Haversham pursed her spinster's lips. 'I don't think so.'

'When did she write that?' Nick asked.

'1967.'

'Did you know her, then?'

'A little. She was an acquaintance, nothing more. We were not sisters. In any sense. Alice Neel was my friend. She painted a portrait of me too, you know. A nude, believe it or not. I was just a kid, of course.' She let out a tiny birdlike titter. Even to herself, Miss Haversham was not easily pictured in the nude. 'It was not a flattering portrait. Alice never wooed you with her pictures. Even when you were naked she exposed you still further. She showed the weakness, the disappointment, never the ambition or the hope. She particularly liked to paint pregnant girls, but she managed to turn all their bloom and promise into something balloonish and macabre.' She must have guessed what we were thinking. 'I wasn't pregnant, needless to say. But I remember when Alice was painting me she was also doing the portrait of a young actress who *was* pregnant, and who was so lovely to look at, so delicate, a little boyish for some tastes, but wonderfully alive and alluring—'

Nick interrupted. 'What was her name?'

'I can't recall. It was thirty years ago, Nicholas. She was quite well known, though. She was another one who committed suicide. It was that kind of time. Anyway, Alice's painting of her was extraordinary, unless you'd met the girl herself. In real life she was lovely, truly beautiful, luminous – even lovelier than you, Miss Macdonald – but in the picture her little bump was all distended like a bladder full of water and her tiny breasts were all lopsided like avocados.'

'What happened to the picture?'

'It disappeared. So did the one of me. Flora commissioned them both, so I suppose they were hers to do with as she pleased.'

'Who is Flora?'

'Flora Whitney Miller. This is her museum. Or, rather, it was. Her mother founded it, but it was Flora who kept it alive, who made it grow. I used to work for her, as a sort of companion and adviser. She was a remarkable lady, absurdly rich, with wonderful taste and an impeccable eye. We were very close, but I'm afraid she didn't take to Mr Rogers. That's why we fell out. She was old and stubborn, and I was young and stubborn. She may have been right about Mr Rogers, but I didn't think so at the time. She made me choose. I made my choice and I never saw her or spoke to her again. After she died – she must have been nearly ninety by then – I came up to New York for the sale. She had the most spectacular private collection, quite separate from the museum, paintings, prints, silver, jewelry, clocks, tapestries, an extraordinary Roman sarcophagus. Of course she sold a lot of the best stuff while she was still alive, the Manet, the Turner, but it wasn't the best stuff that interested me. I came to the sale to see if my portrait was in it. It wasn't. There was everything else I expected to see, except for about six items, six of her favorite pieces, including the two nudes by Alice Neel. They'd gone, vanished, but since apparently they'd never been cataloged and the sale raised millions anyway, there didn't seem any way to take the matter further.' She was still gazing intently at Andy Warhol's wounded torso. 'My life has been full of intriguing little culs-de-sac.'

I broke the silence. 'If you don't mind me asking, what brings you here now?'

'I always come whenever I'm in New York. Without fail. Flora was a kind of mother to me, so it's like coming home. But there's more to it than nostalgia, Miss Macdonald. If you decide to continue your career as a teacher you will find it is very necessary to keep your mind alive, particularly if your school is based in Hicksville, South Carolina, as ours is. Teaching the same kind of kids the same kind of thing semester after semester can harden the heart, etiolate the soul and dull the mind. Half an hour in here is quite a restorative. Have you seen the new Georgia O'Keeffe?'

Nick looked as if what he might have seen was a ghost. He was suddenly pale, and short of breath. 'Would you two ladies excuse me? I've just realized there's something I need to do.' He glanced at his wrist, as if checking the watch that wasn't there. 'Kirsty, I'll meet you at the hotel at six. In the lobby. Okay?' And then he was off. He ran, lightly, quickly, I knew not where, I knew not why.

'Strange boy,' said Miss Haversham, not unkindly.

'I don't really know him that well.' (Was I denying him because I was hurt? Or was I simply telling the truth?)

'I believe it's not unusual for people to fall in love with people without really knowing them. Theo Quincy says it's the only way.'

'What do you think of him?'

'Of Theo?'

'No. Of Nick.'

Miss Haversham turned towards me. She didn't look

at me, but stared down towards my feet. A lifetime of shyness meant that now she never caught anyone's eye. The only time she looked another human being full in the face was in a picture. I doubt if she even confronted herself in the mirror. If, accidentally, unavoidably, the path of her eyes momentarily encountered yours she glanced away at once, confused and alarmed. It was the saddest thing about her.

'What do I think of Nicholas?' She paused and smiled and lifted her head very slightly. 'I think he's quite wonderful. And enigmatic. Like an O'Keeffe. Come.'

She marched me along the museum's bright pine corridors, past light and shade, past ebullient Jackson Pollocks, past seminal Edward Hoppers, past the tangled webs of Louise Nevelson, past Mark Rothko (past his prime), down a sepulchral stairwell, and another, and into a small space dominated by a single canvas, engulfed in light.

'What do you think?'

'It's sensational.' It was. And difficult to describe, Misty. The right-hand side of the picture was like a black holocaust, a great coal-colored swirl of cloud, a nuclear mushroom viewed from above, with at its epicenter a pentagonal starburst of pink and carmine and silver-gray. On the left of the picture, in shades of dazzling blue, were gigantic exotic flowers eclipsing a distant sky of fluffy white clouds and pale lapis lazuli.

'"Black Hollyhock with Blue Larkspur". That's what it's called and that's what it is; that's all it is, according to Georgia. She painted it during her first summer in Taos, New Mexico, in 1929 or 1930. But what do you think, Miss Macdonald? It has to be more than a magnified flower arrangement, doesn't it? But what? Some say it's simply nature aggrandized by art, others say it's symbolic of female sexuality. You pays your money and you takes your choice. In this case, you pays around two million dollars.'

'What do you think, Miss H?'

Miss Haversham stared into the starburst. 'I think . . . I think I don't know. And I believe I don't need to know. We can see it's amazing and beautiful and passionate and powerful and delicate and—'

'And indescribable.' I wanted to laugh.

'I was going to say unique, but, yes, you're right, it is indescribable. So why can't we accept it as incomprehensible as well? We don't need to understand everything, do we? We don't need to explain everything away. Not everything's knowable, is it? There don't always have to be answers. Kirsty, love Nicholas for what he is – the perfect stranger.'

Thirty minutes later I was standing in a corner of the lobby of the Chelsea Hotel talking to a stranger who was far from perfect. In truth I was not talking to him, and certainly not talking with him. He was talking at me, as though I were a simpleminded and delinquent child and he was the oldest, and by far the wisest, of the Three Wise Men. Most of us think we know it all at eighteen and, as the years roll by, realize we know less and less about more and more until eventually we pass out of this world in the sure and certain knowledge of fuck all. Not so with David Hofmann. Solomon and Socrates, in all their magisterial glory, Sandor Ferenczi and D.W.Winnicott, in all their collected papers, had not his breadth of knowledge, his depth of experience, his mind-blowing sense of certainty. Doubt had not been packed in the knapsack of his psychology. He knew he was right and that was that.

'I know what I'm saying, Miss Macdonald. I know what I'm doing, and it's for your own good. And for his, of course.'

'But you've never met him!' Why was I bothering to protest? I was trapped.

'I know enough.' He was bald, but not crudely uncomely because what hair he had was neatly groomed. He was probably no more than fifty, but his manifest complacency gave him an older manner and a younger look.

'How do you know "enough"? From what Prof Atkins told you?'

'From what Professor Atkins has told me, yes; from the way you are behaving now; and from a lifetime's experience in the field of psychiatric medicine.'

'You know nothing.'

'Let me be the judge of that.'

'Why the fuck should you be the judge of anything? Who are you to be sitting in judgment? Why the hell are you here?'

'I'm here because an old friend of mine happens to be an old friend of yours and he's concerned that this young man, about whom you know so little we could say you know almost nothing, appears to betray symptoms of schizophrenia. It could be the mildest schizoid behavior, your friend could simply be an endearing eccentric, a classic schizothymic; but equally and, naturally more disturbingly, it could be a case of hebephrenia – with all that that implies.'

He was winning. This didn't surprise him. He took winning for granted.

'It could also be nothing,' I said.

'Indeed, but, from what I have heard, I doubt it. And I imagine you doubt it too.'

'Leave me alone. Please. Please, go away.'

'You're a sophisticated woman, Miss Macdonald. That's a reaction, not a response.'

I said nothing. I had nothing left to say.

The round, smooth face offered a supercilious smile. 'I'm here to help.'

'I don't want your help.'

'But didn't you call Professor Atkins?'

'I don't want your help now.'

'But I think you need it now. I believe your friend may need it too. Look—' I thought he was about to touch my arm, but he wasn't one to make mistakes – 'Look, why can't we sit down for a moment, have some tea, and talk this through like professionals. Professor Atkins tells me you were one of his brightest students.' (The patronizing bastard!) I didn't move. Hofmann fiddled with an elegant cufflink. 'Miss Macdonald, this is not a game. You may be at risk. I may need to protect you from yourself. As you will know, there are statutes in New York that can help me do just that, but why should it have to come to that? Why can't we sit down like two rational adults, two trained and experienced professional people, and simply examine the evidence.'

'Go away.'

'Miss Macdonald.'

'Fuck off.'

'Miss Macdonald, I'm going to ask you half a dozen questions about your friend. If you can truthfully answer No to any one of them, I will indeed go away. I promise. But if your conscience tells you to say Yes to any one of the questions, I'll ask you to accept that there may be something amiss with your friend, something out of kilter, something troubling him that needs to be checked out. If the answer's No, I go. If it's Yes, I stay. Do we have a deal?'

I said nothing.

'They're elementary questions, textbook stuff, you'll know the kind of thing. First, is your friend a man who has resisted love, resisted the commitment of love?'

He paused. I said nothing. 'Okay. Is your friend a man who seems unknowable even to friends, if he has friends; is he someone who won't let himself be known?'

He was using his stubby, over-manicured fingers to count out the questions. 'Is he a man who, increasingly, suffers from mood changes – sometimes sunny, full of confidence; sometimes distant, full of doubt; suddenly happy, suddenly not?'

He brought his forefingers together. 'Three down, three to go. These are much more straightforward. No judgment required here. Is he someone who believes he has heard voices, seen a vision?'

I kept looking at him and wondering why I wanted him to be wrong when I knew him to be right. 'And five. Does he believe that in some bizarre, not yet wholly explicable way, he isn't what he seems to be? He may look like a regular guy, but does he actually believe he's really some sort of mythical creature, a saint or even a god?'

How can you love a man you don't know?

'I'm assuming silence means assent, Miss Macdonald, so here's the sixth question. It really ties in with the last. Do you find him showing an unexpected, unfamiliar interest in religion? For example, do you find him quoting the Bible at you?'

Over Hofmann's shoulder I saw Nick moving slowly

towards me. His face was hard, his eyes were narrowed and angry and cold. He smiled a bitter smile and whispered, 'Verily, I say unto thee that this night, before the cock crows, thou shalt deny me thrice.'

'Matthew, Chapter 26, Verse 34,' said Dr Hofmann, taking Nick by the arm.

Chapter Ten

As Hofmann's right hand cupped Nick's left elbow, one bearlike arm in a neat Brooks Brothers suit with a sharp white shirt-cuff and a strong black hand went round Nick's shoulder and another went round mine. Theo Quincy pulled us firmly towards him and purred, 'Where have you two been? The boss needs you – *now*.'

With a politely perfunctory ''Scuse us' and a knowing, dismissive nod, Theo the drill sergeant wheeled us sharply away from the enemy, across the lobby and up the main stairway. He didn't speak and we didn't look back until we had turned the corner and caught sight of ourselves in the mirror on the half-landing – Dean Martin, Sinatra, Sammy Davis Jr, three of the rat-pack on the run.

Freud says (in *Civilization and its Discontents*), 'We are so made that we can derive intense enjoyment from a contrast and very little from a state of things.' This may help explain the sudden, intoxicating, sense of freedom and ease and happiness that overwhelmed me as, together, we fell back against the mirror and began to laugh like a trio of naughty medical students high on illicit nitrous oxide. Tears welled into my eyes as Nick kissed Theo and Theo kissed me, and Nick, attempting to hush his own hysteria, declaimed:

From quiet homes and first beginning,
Out to the undiscovered ends,
There's nothing worth the wear of winning,
But laughter and the love of friends.

'Right on!' cheered Theo, slapping his palm against Nick's.

'At least that wasn't from the Bible!' Suddenly it didn't seem a dangerous thing to say.

'Who's your friend?' Theo asked. Nick looked at me and grinned. 'No, not her. The moon-faced dude in the lobby.'

'Don't ask me,' said Nick, quite cheerily. 'It's some guy Kirsty has an interest in.'

'No, Nick, no!' I protested, but it didn't feel important any more. It was just a game.

'Now, now, you two, no fighting in class.' Theo wagged a remonstrative finger at us.

'How did you know we needed rescuing?'

'How did Tonto know when the Lone Ranger required his services? Some primeval instinct, I suppose, that old black magic that you know so well; probably the slave in me. Besides, I can smell fear at a hundred paces.'

'How come you're here at all?'

'Fate. And the fact that I'm due to meet up with the gang at six.'

'You're here with Dr Browne and Mr Rogers?'

'And Miss Haversham. Yes, indeed. But don't ask. If you two can have your little secret, why shouldn't we have ours?'

The madness and the exhilaration were beginning to subside. Theo checked his watch. 'I'm late already. I must love you and leave you, my children. No more talking to strangers now. See you around. Are you staying till Sunday too?'

'I don't know,' said Nick.

'I'll leave you to sort yourselves out. Remember, nothing matters very much and most things don't matter at all.' Lizard lids half closed his protuberant eyes. He mouthed a kiss and turned lightly on his heels. 'Always glad to be of service. Catch you later. *Ciao.*'

Theo ran back down the stairs. Nick took my hand in his for a moment and held it gently. Then he let go, as though he were dropping a pebble. We looked at each other in the mirror and gave shy smiles; we were awkward; the water was freezing over again. The warm pool in which we had splashed so freely just a moment before was turning icy all at once.

'We need to sort ourselves out, Kirsty.'

'Do we, Nick?'

'Can two walk together, except they be agreed?'

'If that's another line from the Bible I'm going to scream.'

'Why?'

'Because there's a guy down in the lobby who thinks you're a psychopath and you seem determined to prove him right.'

'By quoting the Bible?'

'By quoting the Bible, by hearing voices, by thinking you're some kind of saint.'

'I don't hear voices and I don't think I'm any kind of saint. I don't know who I am. That's my problem – and now I've made it your problem too and I'm sorry for that. All I'm doing is what thousands of adopted children do every year. I'm trying to find out who my parents were. It's not unusual. It's quite normal. If I'd been adopted, I don't think I'd have wanted to do it while my adoptive parents were alive, but since it appears I was abandoned at birth, and no one has adopted me, it seems not unreasonable, almost thirty years after the event, and not unduly hurtful to anyone in particular, to try to find out a little more about where I've come from. That's all.'

'That's all?'

'That's all.'

'But what about you and Santa Claus?'

'Forget all that.'

'Forget all that? How can I forget it when you believe it?'

'It's all in the mind. I know. "There's nothing either good or bad but thinking makes it so."' He laughed, and with his knuckles gently, playfully, stroked my cheek. 'Don't worry, that's not the Bible.'

I moved away. We were wandering down one of the hotel corridors, past doors that looked identical leading to rooms that were identical, inside which similar folk with similar lives were watching the same TV shows and eating comparable club sandwiches in varying but limited states of hope, apathy and despair. As Prof Atkins liked to say, 'The diorama of human emotion is superficially colorful but on close inspection alarmingly circumscribed. Keep your ears, eyes and mind open and within a very short while you'll have experienced it all. We poor mortals look much the same because, fundamentally, we are much the same.' But, Misty, Nick Saint was different. He was way beyond my experience. I suspected he was beyond Dr Hofmann's too.

We reached a door marked 'Staff Only'. Nick pushed against it. 'Let's take the service stairs. We can escape out the back. Are you coming?'

'Where are we going?'

'Over the rainbow.'

'Nick, I'm frightened.'

'I know. I'm a little scared myself. That's why I want you with me. I've been waiting to make this journey all my life, but I didn't dare go alone. For years down at Magnolia Hall I've been dreaming my dreams, biding my time, waiting for the moment. And then, that day you came, I thought, "Yes, with her I could do it. Alone I couldn't, but with her . . ."' He had his hands around my neck and with his thumbs he pressed so gently up against my throat. 'Trust me,' he whispered.

'I trust you,' I said. He didn't kiss me. He smiled. I frowned. 'Where *are* we going? Seriously.'

'Seriously, we are going to church, Miss Mac. Believe it or not, we are going to the little church of St Nicholas. It's not far.'

It turned out to be the Romanesque church, on the corner of Tenth Avenue and West 22nd Street, where we had stopped off in the morning with Augustus St George on our way to the Cathedral of St John the Divine. While I had stayed on at the Whitney with Miss Haversham, Nick had checked out that the last service of the day would be compline at six-fifteen and that the celebrant would be the priest-in-charge, Father Sebastian Hemingway.

Perhaps it was Hemingway he looked like, after all, not Walt Whitman. I tried to resist the thought that he looked like Santa Claus, but, of course, he did. Mercifully, not the Clement Clarke Moore version, the 'right jolly old elf' with cheeks like roses, nose like a cherry, chubby and plump, with that 'little round belly that shook when he laughed like a bowlful of jelly'. Not the Christmas card caricature, but something altogether grander, taller, stronger, straighter – more saint than sprite, more nineteenth-century German print than twentieth-century Disney cartoon, more hero and leader than genial Jack Frost cum favorite uncle.

It must have been a little after seven when we let ourselves in to the church. As we stepped across the threshold into the gloom, the sound of the metal latch as Nick lifted and lowered it was like a muffled gunshot that echoed and reechoed on the far side of a frozen lake. In the street it had been dark and cold. In the church it was darker still, but, oddly, quite warm. A fragrant haze of incense filled the air and, as our eyes settled, we saw a distant glow of ocher light seeping from a side chapel off the chancel. We moved towards it, softly, lightly, as though we were stepping through freshly fallen snow. In the chapel itself, framed by a rounded arch of rough stone masonry, standing alone by the altar, holding a lit taper to a golden candelabrum, was Father Sebastian, a perfect Giotto icon with lighting by School of Rembrandt.

He didn't turn to acknowledge us but, when he spoke, his voice, measured, strong, clear, was full of warmth, welcoming, almost amused, teasing even. 'I know you're there, Nicholas. But who is the young lady? Won't you both come out of the shadows and light a candle with me?'

We stepped up the marble step into the little chapel and he turned and looked at us with dazzling blue eyes and a matinée idol smile that drenched you with instant, absolute, all-encompassing, no-resisting, rock-solid-gold star quality. He handed Nick the taper. 'I always light a candle for you, Nicholas, on your feast day. This is your church. This is the chapel where we set out our Christmas scene each year, where I hid you in the crib on the night you were born. This is the scene of your nativity. Welcome home, my boy.'

As I took the taper from Nick to light a candle of my own, the two men embraced. They hugged one another hard, Nick clinging to the oak of Father Sebastian, the priest giving strength to the sapling. Old and young, man and boy, father and son, it was good to see, good to be part of.

'This is Kirsty Macdonald, Father. She's been helping me find out who I am, where I've come from . . .'

'She'll be helping you find out where you're going, too, I wouldn't be surprised. She's even lovelier than I imagined her to be. I hope, wherever it is, you go together. It would be an honor to officiate at your marriage. When the time comes, don't forget I offered. I'll waive the usual charge.'

With one hand he took the taper from me, with the other he lifted my hand to his lips and kissed it with considered courtliness. God knows, it was unreal, but it didn't seem corny at the time. 'Welcome to the little church of St Nicholas. If ever you need a sanctuary you will always find it here. This church is unique in New York, you know. It isn't old as it looks, it was built in the thirties, but it is very special. We only have candlelight here. The organ may be electric; the sound system is state of the art; the heating is oil-fired; we even have the luxury of air-conditioning in the vestry; but we allow ourselves only two forms of illumination – from heaven, through a glorious clerestory up over there – you can't see it right now – and from these small candles, the frail, flickering symbols of our faith. They lighten our darkness, they warm our hearts, yet they are so easily snuffed out. They are important to us. You two must come to our St Nicholas service. Six o'clock on 6 December. The church is full to bursting. We give each kid that comes a candle to take home for Christmas. And I tell them that, on Christmas Eve, every child in the world should light a candle and put it in the window so St Nicholas knows where to come.'

He extinguished the taper and put his arms round our shoulders. He was a big man, no taller than Nick (who was around six foot two inches), but broader and heavier. 'Where will you two be on the sixth?'

'Back at school,' I said.

'Of course.' The candlelight was dancing in his eyes. He smiled. 'The Thomas Browne Academy for Boys.'

'You know it?'

'I don't know it, but I know a bit about it. All the old values, a wonderful setting and a fine faculty – or so they say. I know quite a bit about Nicholas, of course.' He looked proudly at Nick and then turned a steady, playful gaze on me. 'But you, Kirsty, I know all too little about you, except that I'm given to understand that you're a psychotherapist with a secret. Is that right?'

'Who told you that?'

'William Rogers.'

Mr Rogers! Oh, shit! Was Father Sebastian going to turn out to be in league with the devil? Was he going to prove to be a murderer after all? Were we simply being charmed by a monster, seduced by the antichrist?

'I've known Mr Rogers a few years now. And the others. Dr Browne, Mr Quincy, Miss Haversham. I've always wondered what her real name must be. Do you know?' He was looking at Nick again.

'No, I'm afraid I don't. I don't know anything. To be

honest, I'm quite confused. I don't know how you know these people.'

'We have an interest in common, and a common interest – in you, Nicholas, among other things. They talked about you right from the start, right from the time you first arrived at the school, but it was only after a year or so, more like two, that I began to register that a benign providence was deliberately handing me pieces of an unimagined jigsaw. Gradually, as it fell together, amazing piece by amazing piece, I began to think it might be you, it *must* be you; the more they told me, the more like her you seemed. Eventually I realized that it was, it *had* to be you, and once I was sure, once I knew that Charlie Richards' little boy was safe and sound and working his own kind of miracle down in South Carolina, I thought, "I'll go and see him, it would be good to see him, my little St Nicholas." And then, well, and then I thought better of it. I thought, "No. When he's good and ready, if that's what's meant, he'll come and find me." And here you are. The Lord works in a mysterious way his wonders to perform. His timing is like Charlie's used to be – matchless, ineffable, never wrong. How I loved that woman!'

'Did you kill her?'

'Good God, no!' He burst out laughing and the laugh rolled magnificently around the dark deserted church. 'Could I have saved her? Now that's a different question. But, did I kill her? Did I kill the loveliest girl the world has ever known? Did I kill the only person I've ever truly, truly loved? Did I kill Charlotte Richards? No, no, no!' He spun round and faced us, the candlelight now ablaze in his brilliant eyes, a firm hand rock steady on each of our shoulders. 'Guys, I know who put that insane idea into your innocent young heads. It was, it can only have been, that old fat fraud, Augustus St George. God, what a charlatan! Now, *his* real name I do know. I saw you with him this morning at the cathedral. I wondered what mischief he was up to. He always was impossible. And ridiculous. And, without knowing it, a little dangerous. A good actor though, better than I was. I bet he told you that, too.'

'He did.'

'He mostly tells the truth. At least he used to. The truth, in any event, as it appeared to him. Poor Gus. We've not spoken, you know, since that night when we both stood here, right here where we're standing now, and in a state of bewildered terror and remorse passed Charlie's baby between us.'

'What happened that night?' Nick looked at the priest. 'Can you tell me everything?'

'I can tell you everything I know, Nicholas. I have been waiting to tell it to you for an awfully long time. It's quite a story.' He pulled us towards him, enfolding us both in his arms, enveloping Nick in love, acknowledging from me a flicker of uncomprehending resistance. 'Shall we do it over coffee? In the vestry we allow ourselves the indulgence of an electric kettle.'

The vestry also boasted an electric light, a single neon tube offering an unkind brilliance that made the small, sparsely-furnished stone-walled whitewashed room feel like a newly decorated police cell all set for its first interrogation. Nick looked so young and vulnerable in the unsettling glare, like a naive boy soldier setting off for the front, with hope and fear jostling in his heart. Father Sebastian retained his authority, even as he made the coffee and set it out for us on the bare trestle table, but in the harsh brightness the aura was diminished and, suddenly, there was something about him that struck me as phony. It was something ridiculous and difficult to place, as though his beard was false or his shoes had lifts in them. I was seeing him now in a different light, but was the difference in him or in me?

'There she is,' he said, setting a small silver-framed black and white photograph on the table. It was a studio portrait of a classically beautiful young woman. 'There's your mother, Nicholas, the loveliest girl there ever was – saving your presence, my dear.' The Rhett Butler in him offered an old-world gallant's obeisance in my direction. He had to be a phony. Clearly Augustus St George, or whatever he was called, had been right all along.

'Charlotte Richards was born around Christmas 1945, the daughter of a soldier and a veterinarian. Randy Richards had been an actor till the war, then he joined up and spent the rest of his career in the army. A professional soldier, something of a hero, Purple Heart in Korea, no less. And something of an intellectual too. Charlie used to call him "the soldier poet". I don't think any of his stuff was ever published; but Charlie knew reams of it by heart. She made it sound good. Her mom was called Virginia, and she came from Virginia, and though she trained as a veterinarian, which was quite unusual for a girl in those days – she was a vegetarian too, which was even more unusual for a girl from Virginia! – I don't know if she ever practiced, or for how long, or where. Charlie said they spent most of her childhood traveling the world with the army. The Far East, Germany, the Pacific. Charlie said she liked Hawaii best. She maintained that not only were Randy and Virginia the world's best parents, but that hers had been the perfect childhood, *the* perfect childhood. She used to say, "When people speak of the Good Old Days, well, the days of my childhood, those are the days they are speaking of." Charlie went to all sorts of schools in all kinds of places but her dream, her goal, always, as far back as she could remember, was to be an actress. Acting was in her blood; she knew it, her parents knew it. I don't know whether they liked it or not, but they went along with it. They had no choice. I've no doubt Gus told you all about the Barrymore connection.'

We said 'Yes' together, and Nick said it so eagerly, he was so hungry for more. Was Sebastian credible or incredible? How can you tell?

'Did Gus also tell you the story of how we met Charlie? It was *Romeo and Juliet* – known that season, and for all time, as far as I'm concerned, as *Tybalt and Juliet* because when Charlotte Richards and I set eyes on one another, the *moment* we set eyes on one another, we fell in love. It was as simple as that, and as complicated. This is the bit Gus didn't tell you about. He didn't know, or, if he did, he didn't understand. Our love affair lasted five years. As a matter of fact, from where I'm standing, it hasn't stopped. It won't. It can't. I've had thirty years to think this one through. I know what I'm speaking of. I knew then, too. I knew we were destined for one another, it was in the stars. But I knew too that there was something wrong – not something missing, something wrong, something in the way. Ours was a great romance, make no mistake. It was Dante, it was Keats, it was Cole Porter. It was golden. Charlie Richards wasn't just a beauty, she was an intelligence, she was a phenomenon; she was a spirit that took your breath away. But she wasn't a free spirit. There was something that held her back. She knew it, she felt it; she couldn't define it, she wouldn't define it.

I used to think it was fear of madness, of going crazy like old Maurice Barrymore. She kept leaving me, we kept leaving one another, but then we came back, again and again, and it was always wonderful. We'd look into each other's eyes and we'd be inside each other's heads. I am you, you are me, we are one. It was ecstasy, it was as near as you get to heaven on earth, but in the middle of it – no, not at the heart, but gnawing at the edge – was something that was wrong, some doubt, some barrier, some secret, something. If I couldn't have Charlie Richards completely and utterly and wholly and now and for all eternity, I made up my mind: I'd let go. I'd let go, and commit myself to Christ. Gus and the rest, they mocked it and knocked it, but I had a vocation and I followed it. With Charlie I flew. We flew together, we flew so high, we were Peter Pan and Wendy. But there were strings attached. With Christ there are no strings attached. You don't fly, you float. And there's no free fall.'

'What about free love?' Why did I say it, so archly? Why did I say it at all?

'Oh, but you are right, Kirsty Macdonald. This was the sixties and Charlie was a child of the sixties, a whey-faced wide-eyed wild child of the sixties. We had the apartment here, she was an actress, a budding star. She met the Beatles at the Plaza, Warhol at the Waldorf. She danced with Bobby Kennedy, just the once. She even shook hands with Malcolm X. She tasted all the sweets of her time, and the bitter herbs.'

'Did she take an overdose?' Nick asked the question, pushing the earthenware coffee cup noisily across the table as he spoke, as if to blot out the sound of his own voice.

'Oh no. It wasn't an accident.'

'It was suicide, then.'

'Never. It may have looked that way, but it was never suicide. Charlie was murdered. I know it. Charlie was murdered by the father of her child. By your father, Nicholas. Nico Barclay killed Charlie Richards quite deliberately. There can be no doubt about that.'

Chapter Eleven

Misty, I don't know that Nicodemus Barclay would have appreciated his eventual position in *They Sold the Twentieth Century*, the second volume in Time-Warner's eclectic encyclopedia of the entrepreneurs of our time. Barclay saw himself as a unique creative force, an original mind, a lateral thinker and heteroclite, but his true genius was for exploitation not innovation, and the secret of his considerable success was not his wayward imagination, which was limited, but a ruthless determination, which appeared limitless. On the whole what Barclay wanted, Barclay got, but whether he would have wanted his entry to be tucked between Homer T. Barcklay (the guy who pioneered the drive-in car wash in the forties) and Stephanie-Jane Barker (the woman who established the market for unisex fragrances half a century later) is doubtful. Nico Barclay was certainly bigger than both. That his entry ran five lines longer than that of Ray Kroc, founder of McDonald's, would have been gratifying to him; that it was just half the length of the hagiography bestowed on the chairman of Microsoft, Bill Gates, would have been galling. Towards the end, Barclay saw Gates not as a rival but as a threat.

According to the book, Nico Barclay was born in 1940

(on the day and at the hour Trotsky was murdered in Mexico, as it happened), the only son of educated but destitute Polish émigrés who, two years before, had fled to the United States to escape the horrors of the Holocaust. Both parents were partial invalids. Nico's mother, Elizabeth, died soon after the boy's birth – exactly how and when isn't given – and his father, originally Nicodemus Barczyk, who had graduated from Warsaw University as some kind of engineer around 1930, now drifted up and down the East Coast, baby Nico in tow, washing dishes, book-keeping, bar-tending, taking work where he could get it, until, in the fall of 1943, he settled in Maryland when he found himself a permanent job, with accommodation, as the resident manager of a small private cemetery on the outskirts of Baltimore. This cemetery was to prove the basis of the Barclay fortune.

In 1956, with his father dying of emphysema, Nico contrived to borrow thirteen hundred dollars from an elderly member of the family whose trust owned the cemetery, and, with additional funds secured from a loan shark, under an assumed name and unbeknown to his benefactress, he then personally acquired the freehold in the cemetery itself from the family trust. Using his father's records, he proceeded to contact the next of kin of all those who had been buried at the cemetery during the preceding five years (about 5 per cent of the grave-holders) and offered them a cash incentive to agree to the removal of their loved ones' remains to a more fitting and permanent resting-place. Within three months Nico had cleared the cemetery, discreetly disposed of the long-gone and recently forgotten (a handful required wholesale reinterment, a number were freshly cremated and laid to rest in the first Barclay Columbarium, but the bulk accepted reburial at sea, apparently without murmur), and established a mutually satisfactory partnership with a respectable local property developer who created a shopping mall, leisure center and apartment block on the ten-acre site. Nicodemus Barclay gave his first interview (to the Business Section of the *Baltimore Sun*) when he was just eighteen. 'We're in the business of taking dead land and making it live again,' he said.

Over the next few years, with his initial partner and then with others, Barclay repeated the formula across the nation, and his success in redeveloping neglected suburban cemeteries led inevitably to other forms of property speculation, starting with the acquisition of redundant churches, tabernacles and temples ('We need a spiritual place in our hearts, not necessarily on the High Street'), and culminating in the transformation of the vast old theaters of yesteryear into the multiplex movie houses of today. ('Like Henry Moore I work with space, but at least what I'm doing makes sense.')

Within a decade Nicodemus Barclay had become one of the biggest property tycoons in America. He was respected too because he portrayed himself as a 'developer with a conscience'. The land he sought was either underused or wrongly used, condemned or contaminated. In the late fifties and early sixties he became involved in major slum-clearance programs in Washington DC, Chicago, Boston and New York. It was at that time that he coined the phrase 'urban regeneration', and it was as part of one of these programs that he moved his head office from Baltimore to Chelsea. Clement Clarke Moore had been the original developer of the Chelsea district, the area now sandwiched between West 14th and 24th Streets, in the 1830s. A century and a quarter later Barclay built the headquarters of his empire on the site of the old Clarke Moore mansion.

Property, lands, bricks and mortar made Nicodemus Barclay a multi-millionaire. What moved him into the billion-dollar bracket was property of a different order, intellectual property. Where once he had been content to own acres and structures, now he wanted to own ideas and images. 'The trouble with land is they've stopped making it. A picture, a symbol, a character, a dream, you can reproduce endlessly and exploit to infinity.' ('Infinity itself is a number I wouldn't mind owning,' he told *Newsweek* at the time when he was negotiating with the US Patent and Trademark Office to register the patent for the 150- and 320-digit prime numbers which enable massive cost-saving short cuts to be taken when decrypting codes.) Though occasionally originating copyrightable concepts of his own (he developed the weather chart symbols used by TV stations worldwide; post-Cold War he franchised the designs for uniform international road traffic signage to the countries of the former Soviet bloc), and now and again indulging himself by marketing products that were no more than personal fancies, some of which worked (Berlin Wall paperweights), some of which didn't (cans of 'Fresh Air from Chernobyl' as Hallowe'en novelties), his real skill was in taking established, universally recognized characters and concepts and developing or adapting them in such a way as largely to remove them from the public domain and allow them to become the exclusive property of his own private company, the Copyright Consolidated Characters Creations Concepts Corporation, the 7 Cs. ('Only six Cs? So I exaggerate a little? I'm a salesman.')

From the colors of the rainbow to the red heart as a cipher for the word 'Loves', from Alice in Wonderland to Roosevelt's original Teddy's Bear, from the portraits of presidents to the tribal dress of the great Hunkpapa Sioux leader Chief Sitting Bull, from Michelangelo's Head of Adam and Leonardo's Mona Lisa to the yoyo, Barclay found ways of securing rights, and subsequently earning unbounded royalties, from images that, in some way, shape or form, touched 'the heart, mind or spirit' of the public at large. He boasted that he always looked to the future (in the 1970s he secured the prospect of a tidy sum by registering a multiplicity of computer-generated business names incorporating the words 'Twenty-first Century'), but he made most of his serious money recycling the past. 'Nostalgia is the most potent emotion of them all: your yesterday is my tomorrow.' Quite early in his career he started to buy historic houses and open them to the public. Occasionally he bought houses that were just old and provided the historic element himself. Later on he went for the very stuff of contemporary history, acquiring movie libraries, record libraries, the archives of newspapers, kids' comics, news agencies, ad companies. He did deals with museums and galleries around the globe, from the Louvre to the Hermitage, tying up the digitization rights to the cultural heritage of the western world. 'The future is the use of digital images by millions of consumers instead of tens of thousands of businesses. 7 Cs is creating a visual bank of every memorable, every meaningful image known to mankind. The history, lands, peoples, arts and culture of the planet will soon be available to every schoolkid on earth, and each time they take a peek old Nico Barclay will turn a cent or two.'

The only competition Barclay had was from Bill Gates and Corbis Corp. When Nico heard that Gates had acquired Jacques-Louis David's archetypal portrait of

Napoleon, 'Bonaparte Crossing the Great St Bernard', he dismissed it as vanity. ('He just needs something to put on the wall at his shack in Seattle. I already have Tintin and Titian at my weekend place.') When, in 1994, Gates secured the Leonardo Coda, Barclay accepted he no longer had the field to himself, and when word reached him, a year or so later, that the mighty Bettmann Archive, repository of sixteen million of the most heroic and haunting images of the century (Winston Churchill giving his victory sign in 1945; the naked Vietnamese girl running towards the camera in agony after being hit by napalm), had fallen to the youthful computer software king, 'poor Nico' began to feel his age – and lose his touch.

There were rumors that, towards the end of his career, Barclay was planning to break out of the traditional intellectual copyright business, diversifying away from images of past and present and investing heavily into what, in his last published interview, he described as 'Nico's feelgood culture for tomorrow'. 'I am exploring ways of using the computer screen to change the way you feel about yourself and the world in which you live.' In his final years the tycoon, who had once been a noted party-goer and socialite and who would rarely decline an invitation for a media interview ('I'm always ready to soundbite the hand that feeds me'), became notoriously reclusive, somewhat in the tradition of Howard Hughes (see p.287 of the encyclopedia), and the mystery of Barclay's eventual disappearance provoked comparisons with the death in similarly suspicious circumstances of the British publisher Robert Maxwell (see p.452). At its peak, Barclay's personal fortune was estimated at being in excess of $20 billion. He was unmarried.

'If that's whose son I am, perhaps I don't want to

know.' In the glare of the vestry light, Nick looked quite fragile.

'You still *need* to know, don't you?' I said.

'Do I?' He rubbed a finger lightly around the rim of the coffee cup. 'Who knows? Maybe another dad will turn up in the morning. I've already had three in three days.'

Father Sebastian leant forward and collected up the cups. 'This one's the genuine article.' He turned to the sink. 'I am sorry to say.'

Nick looked up. 'You're sure?'

'Sure I'm sure. But if you need evidence, I can provide it.'

'Then there'll be no turning back.'

'Sleep on it. You've waited all your life. There's really no rush. Meet me in the morning. I've got a service at Trinity church at ten, then I'm clear. Yup, another worthy ecumenical effort. It's halved the congregations and doubled the workload, but I'm sure the Almighty knows what he's up to. Good night. And bless you both.'

We walked back to the hotel holding hands, awkwardly, like schoolkids going to their first Prom. I couldn't think what to say. There are moments when a silence goes on so long it becomes impossible to break it naturally. As we turned into 23rd Street, I said, 'What are you thinking about?' I meant to ask it tenderly, but I knew at once I sounded like a barking school marm.

'I'm thinking about myself, Kirsty, and you're quite right, that's wrong, all wrong – and boring!'

Suddenly he picked me up and swirled me round in his arms. He held me lightly and spun with me, laughing as we turned. From the window of my bedroom at Magnolia Hall I'd watched him at the end of the orchard, down by the great ilex tree, swinging Zanu round and round and higher and higher just as he was swinging me now.

'Away with introspection! It's a vice! It's a self-indulgence!' We stopped spinning. 'Get thee behind me, Santa!' he roared. As we reached the steps of the Chelsea he ran up them, pulling me behind him, as though we were reaching the summit of a sunlit hill at the end of a long lovers' walk on a cloudless, golden afternoon.

'Kirsty,' he said as we marched across the lobby towards the restaurant, 'with your permission, we shall dine in tonight, so that, if we so desire, we can get very, *very* drunk. After our champagne cocktails, I think a white Burgundy would match the mood, don't you? Do you suppose the cellars of the Chelsea run to a Montrachet? I know that Dylan Thomas was a regular, but I'm not sure how committed he was to fine French wines.'

As the captain found us a table and the piano player offered Cole Porter ('It's Delovely', natch), Nick Saint looked at me with wonderful movie star eyes and the most beguiling smile. He was my hero, my icon, my demi-god. 'It's all in the mind,' he whispered slowly, and put his fingers to my lips. 'We're going to have a good time, baby.'

And we did. We had the best of times. All most women ask for in a man is a sense of humor and a flat stomach. And they know asking that much is asking for the moon. And even if you get it, it's usually a pretty pale moon and, given time, it has a tendency to wane. That night Nick Saint was the sun and the moon and all the stars in all their glory. He was heaven on earth. He was handsome, he was happy. He was unselfconsciously courteous. He was kind, he was funny, he was cute. He made me laugh so much he made me cry. There was magic in the air.

And at the table. Nick did tricks. He could make animals out of table napkins. He could balance a knife and a fork and a spoon on a wine glass and make them spin like a windmill. He could move a nickel from behind his ear to under his plate and change it into a silver dollar in the palm of my hand. He could blow out the candles on our table and relight them without touching. He was Merlin. He was Arthur. He was Lancelot. We played those kinds of games.

'Who would you most like to be if you couldn't be yourself?' 'I don't know. I'm happy being me.' 'Who's your favorite author? Don't say Steinbeck. Oh, my God, they always say Steinbeck. Or Scott Fitzgerald.' 'Who's yours? Don't say Charles Dickens.' 'I won't say Charles Dickens. And I won't mention *A Christmas Carol*, I promise!'

He told me stories about Sister Peta and Theo Quincy, but only because I asked. I told him about my parents and Monterey and Prof Atkins. I told him too about my summer with Paul, and I told him about Andrew. I think I said too much about Andrew. Misty, even when you're having dinner with Mr Perfect, watch what you say about your exes.

'Were you very much in love with Andrew?'

'It all seems a long time ago and very far away, but yes. Yes, I suppose I was.'

Nick smiled and raised his glass. 'Here's to love!' The piano player obliged with Irving Berlin: 'Falling in Love'.

'Prof Atkins says falling in love is the failing of our time.'

'Really?'

'We've turned love into a narcotic.'

'Oh dear.'

'Yeah. He says that in the west we're all hooked on a sentimentalized notion of romantic love, "a dangerous fantasy where the ego is dominant", and unless we realize it's just an illusion we're all doomed to disappointment. According to the Professor, romantic love is a designer drug peddled non-stop by movies, by books, by TV, by magazines—'

'By poets and philosophers—'

'No, he's serious, Nick. He says we've taught the world to think you can't be happy unless you're high on love. The problem is when you're not high any longer you're not happy any longer, and that's when the trouble starts.'

'Ah, yes,' said my Adonis, using his right hand and the candlelight to conjure up the silhouette of a goat (or was it a devil?) on the nearest wall. 'Men . . . they're all the same!'

'Not according to the Prof. He says the Hindus have got the right idea. They haven't heard of romantic love. They're never "in love", so they can't fall out of it. They simply have loving relationships. He's got a friend who calls it "stirring-the-oatmeal love" – it's humble and hard, it's human, not heroic.'

'And it lasts.' He rearranged his hands and his shadow-play goat turned into a unicorn.

'It's real, that's the point. Romance is hype. It's a bubble that'll always burst. Anyway, that's what the Prof says. He's doing a book on it. *Coming Down from the Clouds: The Pathology of Romantic Love.*'

Nick ordered the check. 'Neat title. Should be a bestseller. For your friend's sake, I hope it is. But he's wrong, Kirsty. I know he's wrong. Stirring-the-oatmeal's good. But falling in love, that's good too. Romance is good. Can't we have both? Can't we be high for ever?'

As the elevator door closed behind us Nick kissed me, properly, for the first time, and in the mirror I saw the reflection of Dr Browne talking to David Hofmann in the lobby.

At ten the following morning Nick and I joined a sparse congregation at Trinity church for what proved to be a remarkably wordy yet oddly soulless service honoring the memory of the naturalist and painter John James Audubon (1785–1851). We sat in the back pew of the cool church observing the unfamiliar proceedings with the sense that we were viewing them through the wrong end of the telescope. It was all happening a long way away. We had reached the peak of the mountain and were gazing down, into the valley beyond, where a strange tribe was carrying out an alien ritual.

Arms outstretched, head held high, grandly outlined against the fabulous stained glass, Father Sebastian stood before the altar, Atahualpa, last Inca king of Peru, and his voice boomed: 'O Lord, hear our prayers and let our cries come unto you! May our supplications take flight and soar towards you, O God of all creation, as the birds of America took flight and soared under the delicate pen of John James Audubon, late of this parish.'

I wanted to giggle. Much to my relief, Nick did too.

The disparate band of elderly worshippers drifted out, and when Father Sebastian had bid an over-familiar farewell to the last of them, he turned to us. 'Was it banal?'

'It was a bit weird,' I said.

'It wasn't working, was it? Having no one in the congregation doesn't help. You'd have thought the

Audubon Society would have found a few decrepit ornithologists to send along. It was their idea, dammit.' He slapped his hand against the pew. 'God, how I hate these made-up services! We're doing them all the time now. No one knows what's going on and no one seems much to care.'

Nick said something I felt I'd heard him say before. 'They miss the security of known relationships.'

'Don't knock it. When we had the Latin Mass, you could go to church anywhere in the world and be part of the service – part of the *same* service. Maybe Krishnamurti wouldn't agree, but there's a value to tradition. Now, anything goes, and if it doesn't turn you on, you switch off. You weren't turned on this morning, that's for sure. We need the familiar. We need to know where we are.'

'Where are we?' I asked.

He sighed a deep, theatrical sigh. 'And why? Those are the questions.'

'No, I meant where are we now?'

'You mean here? You've not been before? Oh, Kirsty, Nick, my children, this is a landmark. This is one of the oldest churches in New York – the foundation goes back three hundred years precisely. This isn't the original church; that burned down, God knows when – during the Revolution, I guess. This is the third church to be built on the site, the celebrated work of one Richard Upjohn, distinguished founder of the American Institute of Architects. These bronze doors were cast in memory of John Jacob Astor, the second or the third, one of the dynasty anyway. Everyone who's anyone has some kind of link with Trinity church. They're all distinguished or celebrated or something.'

We stood in the porch looking out onto the cemetery

in dazzling November sunshine, gentle hummocks of earth covered with rough green grass, row upon row of traditional gravestones, weatherworn, reassuring, an English country churchyard cast adrift in Lower Manhattan.

'So this is the famous Trinity Cemetery then?' I said. 'It's darling.'

'No,' said Nick. 'This is Trinity *Church* Cemetery. Trinity Cemetery is uptown.'

The priest looked at Nick appraisingly. 'In your part of town, my boy – the St Nicholas district.'

Nick smiled. 'Yes,' he said. 'In my part of town. Shall we go?'

'I'd like that,' I said. 'I've never been.'

'Then you must.' Father Sebastian clapped his hands. 'You shall. If you like old cemeteries, you'll love this one. Not only is it the best, it's where the best are laid to rest. My forefathers included. I shall give you the guided tour. Give me two minutes to change and make the sign of peace with the well-meaning rector and I'm all yours.'

We waited for him, and watched out for a cab to hail, on the corner of Broadway and Thames Street, by the spot where a sunken granite stone is carved with the name of Charlotte Temple. Have you read the book, Misty? It tells the story of a young girl, the granddaughter of an English earl, who eloped with an officer who turned out to be no gentleman. He brought her to America and then abandoned her after the birth of her child. Not so long ago *Charlotte Temple* was one of the most widely read books in the English language.

Don't worry, Nick hadn't heard of it either. 'I wondered who she was,' he said. 'When I was a kid I once walked from here, from this very spot, all the way to Trinity Cemetery. It took all day.'

When Father Sebastian had joined us and we'd landed a cab it took all of half an hour. As we drove along St Nicholas Place, down St Nicholas Terrace, across St Nicholas Avenue, Nick said nothing and when we got to the cemetery itself he let Sebastian do all the talking.

'When I said they're all here, I meant it. The Astors, the Van Burens, the Bleeckers, the Remsens. That splendid runic cross marks the tomb of our old friend John James Audubon.' He stalked from grave to grave, almost jumping from one to the next, like a hardened shrimper negotiating slippery rocks. 'Here's Philip Livingston, he was a Signer of the Declaration . . . And you'll like this one, Nick. Alfred Tennyson Dickens, son of Charles . . . Morgan Dix, he was someone . . . And Madame Jumel. Of course . . . Now, here we are. This is what I wanted you to see. Come. Look. Clement Clarke Moore, July 15 1779 – July 10 1863, scholar and poet.'

We gathered around the gravestone. 'This is the guy who gave us Santa Claus, the guy who wrote "A Visit from St Nicholas". In 1822.'

'My favorite year,' said Nick.

'Mine too,' said Father Sebastian, putting a hand on Nick's shoulder. 'Clement Clarke Moore was my great-great-grandfather, you know. An amazing man. Deeply religious.' He laughed. 'It runs in the family. His dad was a priest too, a bishop no less. They were big shots in their day. But good with it, by all accounts. When CCM inherited the Chelsea estate, he gave great chunks of it away and developed the rest with a lot of care. He was fastidious – not such a fashionable virtue these days. He was immensely learned too, a professor of Oriental and Greek literature. He reckoned his claim to fame should have been his *Compendious Lexicon of the*

Hebrew Language, but it's that one corny verse that's made him immortal. Every Christmas a candlelit procession of little kids and carol-singers comes to lay a wreath on the grave. We were lucky Nico Barclay didn't get his hands on this cemetery or poor old CCM would have been reburied at sea.'

Nick was crouching down by the graveside. 'Yes,' he said, standing up quite abruptly.

'Indeed,' said Father Sebastian, still smiling. 'You didn't come to hear about my forebears. You came to hear about yours. It's a tale that's simply told. He was young. He was rich. He was tough. She was young. She was beautiful. She was frail. He seduced her. That's about the long and the short of it. When she got pregnant, she didn't realize at first. When she found out and told him what had happened, he wanted her to get rid of the baby. It wasn't so easy in those days, but he had the money. Anyway, she wouldn't. Not Charlie. He told her that if she went ahead and had it, he'd abandon her and disown them both. He meant it and she knew it. She didn't doubt it for a moment. That night, the night you were born, the night he spoon-fed her the morphine, he gave her back the ring she'd given him.' He pulled a thin gold band off his finger and passed it to Nick. 'She gave it to me just before she died. I'm sure she meant you to have it. She said it had belonged to her father. Oh, Nick, my little Saint Nick, I loved her so much. So much.'

Chapter Twelve

Nick knelt down again by the graveside. There was an old cracked vase leaning up against the tombstone, filled with fresh freesias, sun-yellow and snow-white.

'I can't smell them,' he said.

'Some people can, some people can't,' I said. 'It's genetic.'

'But I can smell roses and carnations and things.'

'Sure. Freesias are different.'

Nick looked up at Sebastian. 'How do you know he killed her?'

'I know.'

'Did she tell you?'

'No. By the time I got to her, she was too weak. She barely spoke at all.'

'Why did you go to see her that night, anyway? Was it just chance?'

'God, no. She phoned. We hadn't spoken for weeks, months maybe. I'd been in Vermont finishing my studies. I'd only just started at St Nicholas's. I was two weeks in, the new boy on the block, as wet behind the ears as they come. She rang me at the church. I knew something was wrong the moment I realized it was her on the line. She never phoned.

Charlie Richards never phoned anybody. They always phoned her.'

'How did she sound?'

'Odd. Different. Frightened. I said, "What's wrong?" She said, "Nothing." She said she had something for me. She needed to see me. Right away. I told her I had a funeral to do. She said, "Can't it wait?" She made me laugh. I told her it couldn't wait, but I'd get to her as soon as I could. I went about two hours later, and there she was, lying back on her bed, white as a sheet, cradling the baby in her arms, cradling you in her arms.'

Nick tried to straighten the vase. 'Why didn't you call a doctor?'

'She didn't want it. She was too far gone. All she wanted was to say goodbye. I gave her the last rites, I took the ring and then, when I heard the noise on the stairs, I ran.'

'Who did you think it was?'

'On the stairs? Barclay. It had to be him. Before Charlie rang I didn't know about the child, but I'd guessed they were lovers. It all fitted.'

Nick stood up and looked at Sebastian, puzzled. 'Why didn't you tell the police?'

'Tell them what?'

'Tell them that you suspected Nicodemus Barclay of murdering Charlotte Richards.'

'I didn't dare. I had no proof. Besides, I was frightened. To tell you the truth, Nick, I thought they might think I was responsible. It is humiliating to admit it, but I thought they might think I was the father. And I couldn't bear that. Not just because I was now a priest, but because, in my mind, in my heart, I had wanted to father Charlie's child. I had wanted us to be lovers. We could have been. Perhaps we should have been. I hadn't dared. I was a coward when it came to love. And I was a coward that night when she gave me the child. I lacked courage. I always have.' He unbuttoned his coat and began rummaging in his jacket pocket. He brought out his credit-card holder and, with one hand, riffled quickly through the cards, just as Augustus St George had done looking for his faded photograph of Charlotte.

'Here,' he said, passing Nick not a snapshot but a flimsy cutting from an old magazine. 'It's something C.S. Lewis said. "Courage is not simply *one* of the virtues but the form of every virtue at the testing point, which means at the point of highest reality."

'When it came to the testing point with Charlie, my courage was found to be wanting. She asked me to take you, to look after you – so I took you, but not just because she asked me. I was frightened not to take you, frightened of the consequences. I held your little body, Nick. It was all bloodstained. She'd wrapped it in a towel, and I hid it against my chest, under my coat. I clambered down the fire escape and I ran. I ran, clutching you to me, pounding along the streets, utterly bewildered, totally terrified, Charlie lying dead in her room, you living, breathing, newborn in my arms. I did not know which way to turn. As soon as I got to the church, I rang Gus.'

'You and Augustus,' I said. 'You're brothers, aren't you?'

'No,' he said, beginning to laugh; then he stopped. 'Yes. How clever of you to guess. We're brothers who haven't spoken for half our lives. What idiots we are!'

Nick said, 'I don't understand.'

'The psychotherapist does.' Sebastian smiled at me

ruefully. 'I've no doubt she did a paper once on sibling rivalry.' It was my turn to smile now. 'I wonder if she did any work on stupidity. Because that's what Gus and I are, stupid. And stubborn. First we loved each other, then we hated each other, then we denied each other. And we've not exchanged a word, not a word, since that night. At our own mother's funeral we did not speak. Jesus, what kind of priest am I? You're right: typical! I've seen it a thousand times. There are families all over New York, living together, in silence. The TV bleats away, night and day, the radio never stops, there's noise everywhere, endless babble and hubbub, but they don't talk. Husband and wife, mother and son, brother and brother – nothing. I visited an old couple the other night, married fifty years, and they hadn't spoken since the end of the Vietnam War. They had a canary. They talked through the canary. They each told the canary things for the other one to hear. They could not, would not, did not look each other in the eye. It is pitiful. And I am no different. We all have secrets, and Kirsty has stumbled across mine.'

'Sorry.'

'Don't be. I think I should try to face the truth at least once before I retire, don't you? For certain I couldn't face the truth that night with Charlie, the truth of what had happened to her, the truth of what was happening to me. When Gus came, I gave him the baby, I handed over Charlie's child. I passed the buck! Somehow, because he was gay, I thought it made sense! I knew I couldn't keep you. I knew you'd be safe with Gus.'

'I was,' said Nick. 'He took me to a convent on Coney Island, the Convent of the Sacred Heart. I was happy there. The nuns were good to me. I'm grateful.'

'Wasn't there an inquest?' I asked.

'Sure. And the verdict was suicide. Another sixties suicide.'

'But what about the baby? It must have come out about the baby?'

'The coroner came to the conclusion that Charlie, having had the baby unaided and alone, disposed of it, and then did away with herself in a fit of remorse.'

'Wasn't there speculation as to who the father might be?'

'No. Her registered doctor gave evidence, but he hadn't seen her as a patient for almost a year. He'd been prescribing Elavil for mild depression, but not morphine.'

'What about the baby?'

'The trashcans of New York throw up a hundred dead babies every year. Nobody went looking for the baby. The story hit the press just twice and then went cold. "Actress Found Dead" and then, ten days later, "Verdict on Starlet: Suicide". Two paragraphs, one picture, and that was it. End of story.'

In the cab, going back towards Chelsea, Nick said, 'Where is my mother buried?'

'I don't know.'

'And my father?'

'Where Nico Barclay lives, I don't know. He's got several places for sure. I do know where he goes to church.'

'To church? Nicodemus Barclay goes to church?'

'Religiously.' Looking at his knees, the old priest proffered a small, wry smile.

'Where?'

'At the little church of St Nicholas on the corner

of 22nd and 10th. Every Sunday at eleven, without fail.'

That Sunday morning, in the bright November sunshine, at a little before eleven, we stood, like amateur sleuths, hunched against the cold, tensed against the unknown, across the street, watching the congregation arrive. There were many more of them than I had imagined, dozens, scores, and they came suddenly, in cars and cabs, out of the subway, on foot. They came with purpose and climbed the solid stone steps with confidence, acknowledging one another with a casual courtesy that implied a common currency, a mutual recognition that each was the right person in the right place at the right time on the right day. To my surprise there were as many men as women, children too, and all looked easy and assured, characters from a court painting by Frans Hals, smooth and round and certain, their eyes alive, their faces intelligent not vacant, their demeanor eager not complacent. They were dressed without ostentation, comfortably, with a quiet style that was in no way dated yet managed to speak of a more gracious age. Several wore hats, most wore gloves and many carried their own missals, elegant leather-bound editions that had kept them company since their first communion. This was a congregation at ease with itself, on its way to pay its respects to its Maker in the dispassionate expectation that the feeling of admiration was entirely mutual.

'He'll be the last to arrive and the first to leave,' Father Sebastian had told us. 'He never stays for coffee. The moment the service is over, he slips away. He won't speak to a soul and no one will speak to him. He sits in the same pew, on the aisle, seventh row back. It's not reserved for him, but it doesn't need to be. Like royalty, there's an invisible moat around him at all times. No one encroaches on his space. As he leaves, I shake him by the hand, always, and say "Good day", but I don't call him by name. He says nothing at all. If he is aware of who I am, who I was, if he recalls our mutual past, it doesn't register in the way he looks at me. He looks at me directly, right in the eyes, but, much as I've struggled to, I have failed to put a meaningful interpretation on that look. Nico Barclay gives nothing away. It could be he simply doesn't recognize me. We only met two or three times in our twenties and, though he hasn't changed that much, I look different now. You can try to approach him if you want, but I doubt you'll get far. From what I can tell he has a personal bodyguard with him round the clock, but even if he didn't he's got an aura that simply says "Don't get too close", and you don't. There's no going up to Nico Barclay and saying "Hi, Dad".'

At half a minute to eleven the last of the polished congregation disappeared beneath the chaste ornamental arch. The lantern-jawed Dick Tracy by my side put his arm inside mine and whispered, 'He's not going to show.' And, Misty, you guessed it. That was the moment when the deep-blue limousine with smoked windows and whitewall wheels purred around the corner and drew up in front of the church.

Without pause, two men got out. One, lofty, black, broad, with graying hair and lived-in eyes that took in the street and the sidewalk all at once, and the predictable, craggy yet elegant, gait that shouted 'I am the bodyguard, hard and wise, go for the obvious and cast Morgan Freeman in the movie.' The other man was the surprise, the revelation. He was young. Or looked it.

I must have seen photographs of Nicodemus Barclay in the paper, but though I knew the name, the face meant nothing. Don't ask me why, but I was expecting Walter Matthau or Christopher Lloyd or even Spencer Tracy, somebody shambling, eccentric, *old*. I might have settled, I suppose, for Richard Attenborough. But this was something else. This was James Dean. Tall, slim, svelte, lithe. Handsome, so goddam handsome. Looking straight up at the church, glancing neither left nor right, he ran up the steps, swiftly, lightly, and vanished all at once. I caught sight of the impeccable profile, the paradigm of the drop-dead gorgeous, and then it was gone.

Fifty-eight minutes later the limousine reappeared and Nicodemus Barclay stood alone at the top of the church steps, brilliantly lit in the sharp mid-morning sun. He paused, not for the effect (though my God, Misty, there was one), but to take a deep breath. It was that kind of November morning in Manhattan: the air commanded you to take breath. He half-turned to check the bodyguard was with him, said 'Okay, Rocky?', and then ran down the steps as swiftly and lightly as he had arrived. It was as he crossed the sidewalk towards his car that the improbable spectacle of an elderly and disheveled Santa Claus, bell in hand, sack on shoulder, stepped out of the shadows and accosted him.

'Merry Christmas, sir! God bless you!'

In full cry, the alarming scarlet figure shuffled towards him, bell ringing, arms waving, avid to embrace him in a rugged bear-hug. Barclay looked around, as if to see who this unseasonal Santa was really aiming to greet. The bodyguard was already out in the road opening the car door. The Santa now dropped his bag and bell and began to grapple with the great entrepreneur.

That's when we moved in. Nick led the shouting, 'Whoa! Hold it now!' We aimed for the Santa, pushing him back. I grabbed the front of his tunic, Nick pulled his arms tight behind his back. As the old boy struggled and swore, I caught sight of Barclay's face, puzzled, amused, unperturbed. Close-to, his skin appeared much more lined, but it was clear and soft, like crumpled silk. The bodyguard swept his boss into the safe haven of the limousine, slammed the door and came back to us. The Santa was making his escape down the street.

'Some poor crazy old fool,' said the bodyguard. 'It's sad. Thanks for your help.'

'Don't mention it,' said Nick.

'Is that Mr Barclay?' I said, peering towards the car. 'Could we just say "Hi"? I'd love to meet him, just to say "Hi".'

'I'm sorry,' said the bodyguard. 'He's very private.'

'Please.'

'Sorry.'

He was saying it as he moved back to the car, fending us off with practiced hands. The limousine began to move as he clambered in. 'Thank you. Thank you both.' They were gone at once. The whole episode lasted no more than a minute.

'Sorry, kids,' said Augustus St George, straightening his tunic and retrieving his bag and bell from the sidewalk. 'It was a neat idea, but you can't win 'em all.'

The old actor used our suite at the Chelsea to change out of his costume. We had already fixed to meet Theo Quincy and Miss Haversham for lunch and, naturally, since he had taken the time and trouble to travel from Philadelphia to take part in our hopeless charade, we invited Augustus to join us. We did not explain his presence to the others. We just presented him as a friend and told them he was an actor.

'Aren't we all?' said Theo, eyes a-popping, Bloody Mary in hand.

'No, I don't think we are,' said Miss Haversham, half-closing her eyes and tilting her head with a maidenly smugness specially contrived to infuriate her colleague. 'We all know that your life is one long performance—'

'Oh yeah, deep down I'm shallow . . .'

'—but some of us are ready to confront the challenges of harsh reality.'

'Who are you trying to fool now? You fantasize as much as any of us.'

'Dreams are different, and if you know they are only dreams, that's fine. Confusing fantasy with reality is the problem.' She turned confidentially to Augustus, who was looking at her with real pleasure. 'As will become all too evident to you over lunch, Mr St George, our colleague is endearing but he's also a veritable minefield of moral confusion. To be on the safe side, don't believe a word he says.'

'Who wants to be on the safe side? Believe what you like, Augustus – I may call you Augustus? It's such a great name – believe what you *like* and junk the rest. That's the point. I decide what I want to believe and you decide what you want to believe.'

'What about truth? What about empiricism? What about logical positivism?'

Theo banged his glass down on the table. 'What about another drink?'

Augustus appeared as delighted with Theo as he was with Miss H. They were his sort of people – ridiculous, full of words, full of booze, full of fancy, full of *ideas*, not necessarily ideas that were sound or profound or original even, but *ideas* none-the-less. He liked these people because they weren't talking about the weather or politics or the banalities of the domestic round or the price of anything. A conceit came up and they just let it shoot around the pinball machine of their conversation: the line was erratic, the logic was loose, unreliable, but bells rang and the spirit tingled. Augustus liked jazz for the same reason.

'Do you like jazz?' he asked, both because the notion had just popped into his head and because, as he prepared for his second Bloody Mary, it occurred to him that in a moment he might summon up the energy to tell his Dave Brubeck story. Recounting set-piece anecdotes calls for energy, as well as skill and memory, and these people were giving him energy.

'Jazz?' exclaimed Theo. 'What would you say if I told you I was the long-lost son of Miles Davis? Don't interrupt, Miss H! This is a special moment: Augustus and I are in the process of discovering that we are soul brothers! We know the Prince of Darkness, we have heard the Sorcerer, we have drunk deep of the Bitches Brew!'

Miss Haversham pursed her lips. Had she had the titles at her disposal, she'd have said 'So what?' and made some disparaging remark about Freddie Freeloader. As it was, she simply said, 'I am skeptical about the value of improvization.'

'Miles Davis had a certain genius,' said Augustus in mock reproof.

'Or was it an uncertain genius, Mr St George?' Miss Haversham was a little bit pleased with this flirtatious sally.

'What is wrong with improvization?' cooed Theo, eyes wider than ever. 'My whole life is an improvization!'

'Improvization is for the gifted but lazy,' said Miss H very deliberately, perhaps wondering if she should invent an attribution for the aphorism to add to its authority. '"Conception, my boy, *fundamental brainwork*, is what makes the difference in all art." I am afraid we are letting the young get away with far too much. It's not fair on the talented – these days their talent is honed not disciplined. The diamonds still shine, but they don't cut. And the talentless, now, they're simply left to wallow. Do you think it matters?'

'Yes,' said Nick. 'I think it matters.' He did not look to me like a man in the throes of an identity crisis, let alone David Hofmann's incipient schizoid. He looked seriously happy, properly carefree, an ordinary guy enjoying an uncomplicated drink with friends that were true and could be trusted. Nick was blessed with the gift of relishing the moment. Misty, I have spent too much of my life anticipating the future, regretting the past, feeling anxious in the here and now. Nick was mindful of the future, conscious of the past, but he dwelt in the present, he seized it spontaneously. 'I think you're on to something, Miss H.'

'Thank you, Nicholas. I value your good opinion *greatly*.' She glided gracefully through Theo's derisive snort. 'You would much have enjoyed the lecture I attended this morning.' She threw me a tiny smile. 'So would you, my dear. It was at the Metropolitan Museum of Art. Mark Roszak on Dante Gabriel Rossetti and the Pre-Raphaelite Brotherhood.' She confided in Augustus, 'William Morris is my particular enthusiasm. Poor Rossetti was somewhat obsessed with Mrs Morris, which was a nuisance for William and perhaps even for Jane too, but glorious for us because he's immortalized her as Queen Guinevere and Proserpina and the rest.'

'The beautiful people,' said Theo.

'Indeed,' said Miss Haversham.

'Give me the beautiful people,' proclaimed Theo, brandishing his empty glass and waving his menu in the direction of a passing waiter. 'I want to eat with the beautiful people . . . I want to drink with the beautiful people . . . I want to sleep—'

'With a clear conscience,' said Miss H, completing the joke and quickly getting back into the driving seat. 'Rossetti had a trying time with the ladies. His wife was another great beauty, but she died of an overdose of laudanum. The poor man was bereft, had his poems buried with her. He thought better of it later and had her body exhumed and the coffin opened up to retrieve them.'

Nick said, 'My name is Might-have-been: I am also called No-more, Too-late, Farewell.'

'Well done, Nicholas,' said Miss H, primly tapping the tips of her fingers together in a token of applause.

'Wasn't Mrs Rossetti a poet, too?' asked Augustus.

'Christina was his sister. People always get it wrong. These aren't the Brownings.'

'Snow had fallen, snow on snow,' said Nick. 'Snow on snow. In the bleak mid-winter, long ago.'

'Nicholas organizes our Christmas concert at school. It is a beautiful occasion. Carols, readings, songs from the shows. Perhaps we can persuade you to come down, Mr St George, and give us a reading. Wouldn't that be wonderful, Nicholas?'

'It would be great.'

'And it would be a great honor for me, gracious lady,

but, alas, I'm committed to a run in Philadelphia. *Peter Pan – The Musical.*'

Miss Haversham gasped girlishly. 'We must organize a school outing. We shall all go. I would adore to see your Captain Hook.'

'I suspect the audiences at the Met feel the same way.'

Miss H missed the joke, but responded warmly all the same. 'Mr St George, your voice produces one of the richest and most romantic sounds I have heard in my entire life.'

'Two Bloody Marys and she's anybody's!' howled Theo. 'It's time we ordered.'

Miss H skated on serenely. 'Are you always touring or do you get to work in New York sometimes?'

'Rarely *de nos jours*. Today was something of an exception.'

'Have you been performing this morning?' Mark Roszak on Rossetti had been wonderful, but clearly Augustus St George in *anything* would have been *heaven*.

'A sort of cabaret engagement,' said Augustus modestly, with a nonchalantly self-deprecating flick of the wrist.

'Augustus has been helping us,' said Nick. He smiled. 'We were attempting to contrive a casual encounter with the notorious Nicodemus Barclay.' He paused. 'But it didn't quite work out according to plan.'

'Nicodemus Barclay?' Theo leaned forward. 'He was here, half an hour ago.'

'Here? In this crummy hotel?'

'Here – in this crummy hotel – in that very bar – having a drink with those two gentlemen.' Theo leant back and waved towards Dr Browne and Mr Rogers who were hovering at the desk by the entrance to the restaurant. Like Tweedledum and Tweedledee, preserved in formaldehyde, they pottered over.

'Why were they meeting Nicodemus Barclay, for God's sake?'

'I know not,' said Theo. 'You'd best ask the Head yourself.'

Dr Browne and Mr Rogers reached our table. They appeared quite drunk.

'Mr Barclay is a charming man,' said Dr Browne with satisfaction. 'And, clearly, brilliant. And, of course, stupendously wealthy.'

'Stupendously wealthy.' Mr Rogers' lizard tongue darted across a moist upper lip.

Dr Browne was looking at me quite steadily. 'Does he live nearby?' I asked.

'In the very next block. Here's his card. By the bye, Miss Macdonald, I've been meaning to apologize. It was very remiss of me the other night. I forgot to inquire after your poor sister. How is she?'

Chapter Thirteen

We eventually came face to face with Nicodemus Barclay on Sunday 6 December, Nick's twenty-ninth birthday. We were quite charmed by the old monster.

Securing the meeting had called for four telephone calls and two lies – three lies, really, if you include the deception we were practicing on Dr Browne. He had offered no clues as to why he and the egregious Mr Rogers had been having a conspicuous drink with the professedly reclusive billionaire in a public hotel bar, and we offered no fuller explanation of our wish to make a day-trip to New York so soon after the mid-semester break than the need to pay another visit to the bedside of my mythical sick sister on Long Island. Neither Nick nor I asked Dr Browne direct why he had been meeting Barclay, partly because we were reluctant to reveal our interest in the great entrepreneur and partly because we knew the headmaster would have had no difficulty in courteously evading the question.

Dr Browne was one of those fortunate people who have the trick of being able to be open and opaque at the same time. When he needed to speak but didn't wish to convey anything except a willingness to be helpful and friendly, he simply gobbled. His jaw moved, his cheeks filled and he made a curious bubbling, burbling, gurgling sound that was offered as a totally meaningless but apparently comprehensive response to whatever question had been asked or request made. On the whole Dr Browne avoided the necessity of lying, having mastered the art of avoiding saying anything if he was not so inclined.

Too many of the little lies I have told in my life, Misty, have come into being not so much from a need to deceive as a desire to please. Feeling that people want to hear something rather than nothing, I offer up a deceitful invention rather than either confronting them with the banal truth or, worse still, leaving silence in the air. In the case of securing an encounter with Nicodemus Barclay, it was different: deception was the name of the game and there was no alternative to the lie direct. Nick (who, I am convinced, had never knowingly told a lie in his life) now became a committed co-conspirator.

On the morning after our return to Magnolia Hall, using the number on the card Barclay had given the headmaster, I called the headquarters of 7 Cs and asked to speak to the press office. I told them my name was Hannah Ramey, that I was a freelance correspondent for the German news magazine *Der Spiegel*, and that I was looking for an in-depth interview with the legendary tycoon. At once I was told that Mr Barclay no longer gave interviews. I explained that I would be writing the profile in any event, and I was seeking the interview not to intrude on his privacy but to ensure that the piece was as accurate and up-to-date as possible. The press office volunteered to send me a full biography of Mr Barclay, together with a copy of *Success in Quotes*, a thirty-thousand-word digest of the Barclay business philosophy expressed in bite-sized nuggets ('just ideal for your piece') and taken from sources as varied as the Bible ('A little sleep, a little slumber, a little folding of the hands to rest and poverty will come upon you like a vagabond and want like an armed man') and the great man's own epigrammatic small-talk ('Never forget that the winners are only doing what the losers wouldn't'; 'Dream the impossible dream, then wake up and live it'; 'Don't mistake motion for progress; it's the outcomes not the inputs that count').

I said, while I would be pleased to see the material (and asked for it to be sent care of the Chelsea), could I earnestly request that Mr Barclay personally be asked whether he would consider this interview, given the prestige of the publication I represented and the international nature of the audience? In the spirit of a Barclay dictum ('When they say "No" it's maybe; when they say "Maybe" it's yes; when they say "Yes" you haven't asked for enough. That's not always how it is, but it's always how to play it'), I said I would call back in twenty-four hours. When I did so, because the line to the press office was busy, I asked to be put through to Mr Barclay's private office and found myself talking to 'Anita Polo, the founder's personal assistant', who was as helpful as the press office, and as adamant. 'Mr Barclay no longer gives interviews. He feels he has said everything he wants to say.' On the third day, I rang again. I spoke quite briefly to Ms Polo this time. Nick had had an idea of the line to use and I used it, word for word. 'Would you give Mr Barclay this message: the reason I'd like to meet with him is that I want to talk to him about Santa Claus.'

On the fourth day, I called for the last time. 'Mr Barclay would be pleased to meet you. He suggests the first Sunday in December at just after noon at his apartment. Would that be convenient? Let me give you the details.'

When it was built in 1930 the sixteen-story London Terrace building, occupying the full block between Ninth and Tenth Avenues and 23rd and 24th Streets, was possibly the largest apartment house in the world. Set on the site of the original London Terrace and Chelsea Cottages (so fashionable in the middle of the nineteenth century and part, of course, of the great estate settled by Captain Thomas Clarke in 1750), the massive Farrar and Watmough structure, with getting on for two thousand individual homes, a swimming pool, a solarium, a gymnasium, a central garden for the residents and a force of handsome doormen all costumed as traditional British 'bobbies', proved a minor milestone in domestic architecture and, if not quite one of the marvels, certainly one of the curiosities of the age. Go see London Terrace today, Misty, and you'll find the novelty's worn off and the glamor long since gone.

Following Ms Polo's careful instructions we made our way to a nondescript side entrance at the eastern end of 23rd Street and reported to a good-humored security guard who appeared to be expecting us and didn't begin to require us to deploy the ingenious lies we had rehearsed to explain our lack of proof of identity. 'Mr Barclay's just back from church. You can go straight up.' Using a swipe-card, he accessed the elevator and ushered us in. 'There's only one button, there's only one place to go. Enjoy.'

As the mirrored doors of the elevator closed on us, Nick pressed the button, and I said, 'Over the top!'

Nick said, 'Remember the famous last words of General Sedgwick at the Battle of Spotsylvania?'

I said 'No', and the doors opened and there was Nicodemus Barclay. He was smiling broadly. He said, 'They couldn't hit an elephant at this dist—'

'I'm sorry?'

'The famous last words of General Sedgwick. I overheard what you were saying in the elevator. I couldn't help it, I'm afraid. It's amplified – for my amusement. On the whole it's more fun hearing what people say on the way down than on the way up. Let me take your coats.'

The elevator opened straight onto a vast hexagonal lobby, like the inside of a gigantic Art Deco honeycomb. The floor was African marble, the walls paneled with contrasting veneers; the tones were all shades of beige and brown, but the effect was of a golden sunset, rich and warm and life-enhancing. Barclay's charm seemed just like Nick's, unconsidered, effortless and overwhelming. He looked straight at you and his smile filled his eyes and simply made you feel *so good.*

'It's beautiful,' I said.

'Then you'll feel at home here,' he said, handing our coats to the maid. 'Welcome. I'm Nico Barclay, call me Nico. And I take it you're Hannah Ramey.'

'Hannah, please.'

'A lovely name. A palindrome too. And this is?' Quite formally, he extended a welcoming hand to Nick, as though they were tennis players about to embark on a significant semifinal.

'My colleague,' I said lamely. 'I hoped you wouldn't mind.' I felt the color rising in my cheeks. 'Charlie—'

'Charlie Richards,' said Nick, with a slight nod of the

head. He looked steadily into his father's eyes and repeated the name, 'Charlie Richards.'

There was not a flicker of either discomfort, recognition or surprise in the face of Nicodemus Barclay. With his left hand he patted the handshake as a kind of endorsement of his welcome, and said, 'Charlie, Hannah, it's good to meet you both. Shall we go to my study? Coffee, tea, juice?'

'An orange juice would be great.'

'Same here.'

He pushed open wide double doors and led us into his study. Not that I have ever set foot on a seagoing vessel of any kind, Misty, but the room struck me immediately as being a sort of fantasy version of a grand saloon on a luxury liner from a bygone era. There were shallow steps leading down into it and the color scheme was startling: everything was white – walls, ceiling, paneling, drapes, rugs, light fittings, davenport, tables. Even the upright chairs were covered with white leather, and huge white lilies protruded from an elegant white vase on top of the white grand piano whose keys were ivory and cream.

'Cole Porter played the piano, and Syrie Maugham designed the room,' explained our host.

'My!' I said.

'From the grave, alas. She died when I was fifteen, but when I came here I felt this room needed her touch, so I shopped around for it. Everything you see, bar the pictures and my desk, was acquired for clients by Mrs Maugham, mostly between about 1930 and 1935. It took me three years to get it all together. Starting was easy. We can all be starters. It's the finishers who count.'

'As you say in your book.'

He bowed a grateful acknowledgment towards me. 'As you can tell, Hannah, Mrs Maugham was into white in a big, big way. As an interior decorator, it was her trademark, I guess. She was a remarkable woman – from a remarkable family. Achievers one and all, and each with their own territory, their own trademark, their own brand name, even. Her father was a noted philanthropist, British. Dr Barnado was his name. He started homes for orphans and kids who'd been abused. Her first husband was Henry Wellcome, the king of pharmaceuticals, and her second was Somerset Maugham, who walked with a squeak, but you can't win them all. He was a lousy lay, but, boy, could he spin a yarn!'

Nick had moved further into the room and was standing by the chaste ornamental fireplace gazing up at a portrait of a striking-looking woman dressed in a white beaded evening gown with an almost comical coiffe of pale ostrich feathers in her hair. 'Is this Mrs Maugham?' he asked.

Nico Barclay laughed and went to join Nick, putting his arm comfortably over his shoulder. 'Heavens, no! Syrie Maugham had many attributes, but, sadly, physical beauty was not among them. As you can see, I have pictures of only beautiful women on my walls. That, Charlie, is Mary Pickford, sweetheart to the world. And here—' He moved Nick on to the next painting – 'this is Alice Joyce. Mean anything?'

'No, sir.'

'It did once. Alice Joyce was one of the great stars of the silent screen. *Womanhood*, 1917, made by the Kalem Company in their studio on this very block, 235 West 23rd Street. Oh, yeah, when Hollywood was still in short pants, we were making class movies in Chelsea.' He stepped away from Nick for a moment and looked slowly about the room. 'Every one of these fabulous women is an actress in one way or another associated with this part of town.

Until World War One this is where the studios were. Mary Pickford made *Good Little Devil* here on West 23rd, in the studio on the top two floors of the old armory building.' He took Nick by the arm and steered him across the room. 'This is Lillie Langtry, the legendary Jersey Lily, mistress to King Edward and sometime neighborhood beauty.' He spun round and pointed to what must have been the largest painting in the room. 'That's Sarah Bernhardt, the divine Sarah, none greater, by all accounts. She lived at the Chelsea for a while, you know. I've got 'em all in my collection – ancient and modern. Come see.' He led us to the far end of the room, to what looked like a second piano but turned out to be a desk. 'Theodore Dreiser wrote *An American Tragedy* at this desk. He was a fool. But never mind him, look at this.' He picked up a small silver frame that contained a delicate line drawing. 'Drew Barrymore by David Hockney commissioned by Nico Barclay,' he said with pride. 'She's cute, isn't she?'

'Who's this?' asked Nick.

On the wall immediately behind the desk-piano, unframed, unlit, was a large canvas of another beautiful girl. It appeared to be the only nude in the collection. Nico Barclay replaced the line drawing and looked up at the painting. 'Alice Neel,' he said.

'Isn't that the name of the artist?'

'Yes. It's not really part of the collection. It's a case of "artist notorious, model unknown", I suppose. I think I acquired the picture for reasons of gallantry. I wouldn't want it to be on public display. It's not very flattering, is it? I'm sure the young lady must have been prettier than she's painted. Come!'

He swept us back to the center of the room as the maid appeared with the orange juice, bright red. 'We use only blood oranges. I hope that's okay.' He indicated the huge couch. 'Please. Let's sit. Make yourselves comfortable. You didn't come here to learn about my fondness for beautiful young women—' he smiled – 'though it appears, Charlie, it's a trait we share. You came to talk about Santa Claus.' He poured the juice into the glasses and handed it round. After a pause he looked at me steadily, apparently amused. 'How did you find out? That's what I want to know.'

'Sorry?' My heart began to pound so hard it hurt.

'I guessed you might be on to something when you showed up with that ridiculous old Santa outside the church the other Sunday, but how? How did you know? Who could have told you? It's my big secret. Rocky's the only other one to know. You couldn't have guessed, and Rocky didn't tell you. So how?'

Oh, Misty, all at once I was much too far out and not waving but drowning, not even flailing but suddenly, utterly engulfed by the waves. I couldn't breathe.

Nick leaned forward, looked at his father quite calmly and asked, 'Is it true, then?'

'Oh, it's true all right,' said Barclay, setting down his glass. 'It's true.' He grinned. 'And I think you'll agree, it's fantastic.'

'Sure,' said Nick, almost in a whisper.

'It's going to be huge, nothing bigger. It's going to get coverage, massive coverage. And it's going to get out that it's me. That's fine. But not yet. It's too soon. I'm not ready.'

'When you say it's you—'

'Don't worry, guys. You can have the story. It's your story. And to launch it in Germany is perfect. The Germans virtually invented Christmas, for God's sake. So long as I'm on the cover, it can be a *Der Spiegel* world exclusive. That I guarantee. It's all yours, no question. Nico Barclay's last-ever interview. Nico Barclay's greatest coup. You'll have it. But you'll have it when I'm ready. Not before. Do we have a deal?'

I began to laugh. I had taken the wrong turning. I had passed the dangerous corner. I had seen a ghost that wasn't there.

Nick took a pencil from his pocket. 'When could we run the story?'

'Don't write anything down, Charlie. We haven't done the deal.' He got to his feet and walked over to the fireplace. 'Early spring, around the time of the Toy Fairs. That'd suit me nicely. Santa Claus on the cover of an international news magazine in February. That'll make 'em sit up. Nico Barclay does it again.' He punched the air with pleasure as much as pride. 'Oh, my God, they'll kick themselves and say, "Fuck me, why didn't I think of that?" It's so easy, it's so obvious – the greatest character-merchandizing opportunity the world has ever known. And I'm seizing it.' He grabbed a handful of air and pulled it tight to his chest. 'It's the ultimate – the complete ownership and proper branding, marketing and management of Santa Claus.'

It was a declaration inviting applause. Perhaps Barclay seemed so easy because it was so long since he'd been crossed. When he approached a door it opened, when he asked he got, when he smiled the world smiled back.

'Congratulations,' I said.

'Thank you, Hannah. You've read the book. You know the line. "Every proposition is preposterous to those who wouldn't dare." I dare, and he who dares, wins. This is the greatest myth the world has ever known and I'm claiming it for myself.'

'How exactly?' My Superman was in his Clark Kent mode, on the edge of the couch, pencil in hand, not so much the ruthless investigative journalist as the innocent reporter at large.

'The usual way. Santa Claus is just one more product when all's said and done. It's Coca-Cola, it's a Big Mac, it's a Datsun. I'm going to handle this product much as I'd handle any other. Given it's kids I'm aiming at, I've a feeling that my position in the computer games market will be of some assistance.' He took a deep breath and sighed a contented, complacent sigh. 'The product is perfect. The branding is shit. I'm just a marketing man whose day has come. I'm going to play it by the book. I'm going to define my brand, I'm going to establish my brand, and then I'm going to sell it. As simple as that.'

We were looking up at him like wide-eyed children. 'Simple, of course, does not mean easy. If it were easy, they'd all be doing it. You've got to have what it takes. You've got to think it through. You've got to concentrate, hour after hour, day after day. You've got to have the capacity *de fixer les objets longtemps sans être fatigué*.' His accent was nearly perfect. 'Do you two have heroes?' he asked. 'We all need heroes. That's one of the problems these days: not enough heroes. The Emperor Napoleon is one of my heroes. Wise guy. And his brand image has stood the test of time. We all know what Napoleon looks like. We've all heard of Josephine. And we all think of him as a winner, when, in truth, he was a loser, and a big one.'

'Where do you start?' Nick asked the question.

'With the look, always with the look. Eighty-three per cent of any message is appearance and manner. Napoleon without the hat, the Lone Ranger without the mask,

Cyrano without the nose, Sherlock Holmes without the pipe – forget it. There's nothing there.'

'You mean Santa without the costume isn't Santa?'

'Sure. And that's just one of the problems. Santa's costume's cute, the colors are great, but there's no consistency. It's all over the place. In different countries there's a different look. Worse, there's no quality control. What's more, we have a universal character without a universal name. We call him Santa, the Brits call him Father Christmas, the French call him Père Noël, the Germans call him Saint Nick. It's madness. The poor bastard's got half a dozen names and as many birthdays. Today's one of them, you know.'

'Yes,' said Nick, 'I know.'

'Not everybody does,' said Barclay, turning away and shaking his head. 'Let's face it, the myth's a mess, and since no one else has yet gotten round to doing anything about it, Nico Barclay is taking the initiative. Once and for all I'm going to get to grips with Santa Claus and I tell you, Charlie Richards, when I've finished with him he'll make Mickey Mouse look like Howard the Duck.'

'Why? Why, Mr Barclay?'

'The heart has its reasons.' He was looking down into the fireplace as he spoke and he said it softly, almost to himself. He swung round and faced us. He had the most extraordinary energy. 'Santa's what we called "a gateway character". He's so potent to kids that what he says they'll do. Right now he doesn't say much. He says, "It's Christmas and here are some presents." That's it. Well, that's not enough. My Santa's going to say a whole lot more and, when he says it, watch out. If it's blessed by Nico's Santa, you'll want it. If Nico's Santa tells you you need it, you'll have to have it.'

'But what about the other Santas?'

'Frauds and impostors. The deliberate me-toos and the rip-offs I'll sue from here to Armageddon. And the rest won't last. They'll struggle on for a year or two, then they'll disappear. A beagle is a beagle, but only Snoopy is Snoopy. Superheroes come and go, but there's only one caped crusader. Nico's Santa – it's the real thing. Accept no substitutes will be the message. And they won't.'

Nick sat back uneasily. I couldn't tell if he was puzzled or appalled. 'How will you make them believe in your Santa?'

'Believe? What's believing got to do with it? It's not a question of belief. It's a question of marketing. I don't want them to believe. I want them to buy. You're not wearing that tie, young man, as a matter of faith. You're wearing it because every other guy on the planet is wearing one too. It is a totally useless piece of cloth. It is the epitome of the futile fashion accessory. It serves no purpose. It achieves nothing. You're wearing it for exactly the same reason that millions of men around the world wear ties every day of the year. It's something that somehow is expected of them. Someone's told them to do it. It's something they've been *sold*, something they couldn't *not* buy.' He paused, I think to assess the effect he was having on us.

I couldn't work out what it was. I was charmed by him, no doubt, but I was troubled, too. In my naive confusion I asked, 'Why do you go to church?'

He answered without a moment of hesitation. 'Habit. And aesthetic pleasure. I go to Mass for much the same reason as I wear a necktie. It's less commonplace, less fashionable, but it's something I've always done, something I like to do. I'm comfortable with the routine, I like the ritual. And the church itself, the physical space, and the words, their poetry, and the music, the actual sound, they give me pleasure.' With his fingers he tapped his forehead. 'Inside my brain they set off the endorphins. That's the secret.' He moved back to the table and poured out more of the orange juice. 'At the church I go to they've got a good product. That's why it's full every Sunday, while the church on the next block is deserted. Father Sebastian knows his business. And I know mine. And a year from now you can take it from me that every other Santa will begin to look like a sad and sorry relic from a long-lost world. Who wants a pathetic old ragdoll when they can have a brand-new Barbie? By the time I'm through, no one will want a Santa who isn't *my* Santa, the supreme Santa, the only one you couldn't not buy. One name, one look, one dream, one owner.'

'You can't own people's dreams.'

'Who says? It's not written in the stars, you know.'

Nick shook his head. I could tell that he wanted to call out, 'It is! It is!'

Barclay could tell it too. 'Bless you, son, but, with respect, you're wrong. Dreams are all man-made. Nightmares too. I've produced three movies in my time. I know. I've seen how it's done. You need a good script, with a beginning, a middle and an end, and an internal clock that's ticking from the start. The writing's got to be good, but it doesn't have to be for real. It is all a matter of technique. ET was a rubber puppet, you know. It was the music and the lighting and the voice and the artificial tears that made you cry. You were manipulated. It was as phony as the Toronto blessing and as easy to manufacture – if you know what you're doing. I know what I'm doing.'

'Do you?'

'It's my life, Charlie, and I'm writing the rules. Years ago I was interviewed by the *Baltimore Sun* and right at the end the guy said, "What do you want to be remembered for?" And I said, "Ever." Neat answer, eh? Well, now I've found a way. What Barnum did for the circus, Barclay's going to do for Christmas.'

'Why you?'

'Because it's my idea, kid. My copyright. Santa belongs to Daddy.'

Chapter Fourteen

I had known my professor of psychology for just on a year when I learnt that Atkins was not his real name. At the time I was disconcerted by how much the discovery of something so trivial unsettled me. The Prof's parents came from Latvia and the family name was Raudive. In the year he came west and started at college he decided to do so with a new name, 'not so much a more American name as a more neutral name, a name without baggage' was how he put it. He found Atkins in the phone book. There was nothing more to it than that. 'It wasn't euphonious, but it was easy to spell and sent out no obvious signals.'

The Prof volunteered this information himself, quite casually, almost in passing. He had written an essay entitled 'Licensed Behavior: Coming to Terms with Reality' and asked me, the earnest acolyte, if I'd like to read it in proof. I said yes, I was flattered, and he explained that the English word 'license' originated with the fourteenth-century Latvian word '*likt*', meaning 'to come to terms'. Our relationship was already being conducted with a faint flavor of father–daughter flirtatiousness so that when I congratulated him on his familiarity with medieval Latvian he began at once to tell me about his parentage and his change of name. It was no big deal – millions of our fellow citizens have changed their names – but I suppose I was thrown because I felt a bit foolish: my teacher wasn't precisely who I thought he was.

There was also something disconcerting within the essay itself. The Prof was exploring one of his favorite themes: we are subject to a multiplicity of impulses; we keep them in balance by 'licensing' our responses to them. The Prof did his best to practice what he preached. For example (and this was the most eccentric example in terms of his personal behavior), Professor Atkins believed in controlling his temper – except on Saturday mornings. 'It is possible to keep anger at bay, to abate annoyance, to diffuse irritation even, and to do so without damage, by the simple expedient of refusing yourself the license to indulge them on a daily basis knowing that you have given yourself permission to indulge them to the full on Saturday morning.' According to Atkins, this process of 'self-licensing' covers every aspect of our behavior, from the merely social to the profoundly personal, from the conscious to the unconscious. 'At one end of the pool, the shallow end, for example, some of us from a certain generation have no problem in not swearing in front of women because we have given ourselves a license to unbridled profanity in the locker-room. At the other end, the deep end, dreaming, for example, permits each and every one of us to be quietly and safely insane every night of our lives.'

It wasn't so much the idea that troubled me as the way the Prof expressed it. What he said in his essay about dreaming I had read before – quite recently, and word for word – in a work by Charles Fisher. Perhaps, on Sunday afternoons, Professor Atkins allowed himself a brief license to plagiarize.

'None of us is quite what we seem,' said Nicodemus Barclay that Sunday afternoon as he escorted us towards the elevator. 'You seem to be two of the most delightful young people I have had the pleasure of encountering in a long while, but you'll probably turn out to be the Bernstein and Woodward of your generation.' He was walking between us and, lightly, he put his arms round our shoulders. 'I hope not.'

There were two copies of his book waiting on a side-table in the hexagonal hallway and, while the maid fetched our coats, he inscribed one for each of us and presented them, without ceremony. 'Just souvenirs – tokens of esteem, I'm afraid, rather than friendship. I don't mean that rudely. It's simply a rule of mine. Befriend reporters by all means, but never make friends with them. By definition, a good journalist can't be trusted, and I don't want friends who are bad at anything.' He laughed and, as he did so, looked so young and easy. (Perhaps this was what President Kennedy had been like? In build, Barclay was slighter, more wiry, more like Bobby than Jack, but there was definitely something presidential in his manner, a presence that was simultaneously formidable and disarming.) He held out a hand quite formally: it was a post-signing-the-Treaty handshake. 'You've not revealed your sources. I respect that. Run the story in the spring. If you let me see it first I'll endeavor to correct only matters of fact. Goodbye. It's been good.' The mirrored elevator doors began to close. 'Merry Christmas.'

We uttered not a word in the elevator and, awkwardly, studied our own reflections, giving nothing away, both wondering if we were, in fact, on camera as well. When we reached the street, all Nick said was, 'Do you mind if we don't go to the church, after all? I'd like to get back.'

We had tea on the aeroplane and I raised my cup to my handsome, elusive, illusive friend and said, 'Happy Birthday!'

He said, 'I wonder if it is.'

'Come on, Nick, it's been memorable even if it hasn't been that happy.'

'No, I didn't mean that. I wonder if it's really my birthday.'

'It must be.'

'Where's the proof? Where's the fucking proof?' (I'd always been oddly pleased that Nick allowed himself a license to use bad language when we were alone together. It was something he never did with others. It was part of our intimacy.) 'Kirsty, what if the whole thing's just a dream, a frigging nightmare . . .'

'You're wide awake, Nick.'

'Am I?'

A helpful moment of turbulence slopped the hot tea over the rim of the cup onto Nick's hand. 'Yup,' he laughed, 'I'm awake.'

'Do you have dreams? At night, I mean.'

'Sure. Don't we all have dreams?'

'We do indeed, but we don't always remember them. Or want to.'

'I have just the one dream,' he said. 'Night after night. I had it again last night. For as long as I can remember, since I was a kid, it's been the same dream; not every night, of course, and not always exactly the same, but once a week, sometimes more. Around this time of year, a lot more.'

'What happens? Do you want to tell me about it?'

'Sure.' The backs of our hands were almost touching. Gently he tapped his knuckles against mine. 'You've done the training. You can tell me what it all means.'

'I doubt it.'

'If I am twenty-nine today, it's probably about time I shared this with someone.' He lowered his eyes. His eyelashes were so long. 'Actually, it's quite embarrassing.'

Our heads were close. I put my finger to the tip of his nose. 'Don't worry. I'm trained to cope dispassionately with young men and their post-adolescent fantasies.'

He laughed and looked up again. 'No, it's nothing like that. I call it a dream, but it's just a picture, really. It's an advent calendar. And the picture on the calendar is of a wild wood, a pine forest, I suppose; it's dark and green, but even though it's night you can see quite clearly because of the moonlight and the snow. The treetops and the branches are tipped with crystal and there's a carpet of frost on the ground. Somehow a sprinkling of silver dust has been sprayed across the whole scene so it shimmers and glimmers and sparkles. You can feel it with your fingers. The sky's deep blue velvet with tiny shining stars and an alabaster moon. In the foreground there's a clearing and a path marked out with stones leading to a kind of old-fashioned farmhouse, with beams and gables and dormers, almost like a Hansel and Gretel cottage, but much larger, and it's there, welcoming you, glowing, in the heart of the forest. There are candles in the windows, and if you peep through upstairs you can see the kids, gold and brown, black and white, big and small, tucked up in bed, fast asleep.'

'Are you part of the picture?'

'No, never. It's as if I'm floating above it, as though I'm landing in the clearing by balloon and, as I get closer to the picture, that's when I realize it's an advent calendar with little windows cut into the card. And as I reach each window it bursts open and inside there's another picture, smaller but just as clear. Each little scene is fantastic, the colors so vivid. There are snowmen, proper snowmen, with bright orange carrots for noses and round pieces of black coal, shiny and hard, for eyes. There are kids on sledges, kids throwing snowballs, kids with skipping ropes and wooden hoops. There are reindeer, with gleaming harnesses and silent silver sleighbells. There's candy cane and multicolored spinning tops and a giant painted rocking horse with real horse-hair for its mane. There are stockings, striped red and green, stuffed with presents, all neatly wrapped and tied up with scarlet ribbon. There's holly and ivy and mistletoe, and a Christmas tree that is exactly like the one I keep in my room at Magnolia Hall. There's even a window that lets you into Santa's workshop on the night before Christmas.'

'It sounds beautiful.'

'It is beautiful, Kirsty, except for one thing – one window, the last window, the only double window. It won't open. Sometimes in the dream I don't reach it but, even when I do, it stays tight shut. I go closer and closer so that my eyes are right up against the perforations in the card. Through the tiny crack around the casement I can feel the bright light seeping through, but the window won't open for me.' He paused. 'No doubt Dr Hofmann would have the answer. How about you?'

'I don't know. Dr Freud would have told you that pigs dream of acorns and geese dream of maize and that it's just a classic case of wish-fulfillment. But I'm not a Freudian, Nick.'

'What are you?'

'Confused of Monterey.'

'What do you mean?'

'I mean, Nick, that I don't think I can go on with this.

I think I'm in love with you, but, forgive me, I don't believe in Santa Claus.'

Back at the Thomas Browne Academy for Boys the winter semester rolled ding-dong merrily towards a close. Christmas was coming and there was a play to produce, a concert to stage, and for parents, boys and faculty on the last day before the holiday, a Dickensian costume party to organize. Nick was in command of it all, the pied piper of Charleston, the well-mannered Lord of Misrule, master of ceremonies, play-maker, cheerleader, reveller-in-chief. Watching him from a distance he seemed again as he had been when we had first met, in his element, easy, gracious, graceful, careless, kindly, happy, free. It was obvious he loved the boys in a quite uncomplicated way; it was a love that was protective not possessive, creative not encroaching; he loved to be with them, to teach them, to watch TV with them, to play computer games with them, to talk with them, to walk with them, to run and jump and skip with them. He had said to me one night at the Chelsea, it was that first night, when we had bagels with lox and cream cheese and talked till dawn, 'A child of seven moves from A to B with a skip. It's the only way a happy child can get from A to B. Tomorrow look at the sidewalks of Manhattan and see the adults come and go, no skip in their stride, no skip in their heart. We've lost it, Kirsty. The skip has gone. We're all grim, gray, grown-ups now. The millenium's almost with us and the world is middle-aged. We're so damned sophisticated we've even managed to rob the kids of their childhood. If you want to play in the long grass, you can't any more. Innocence has all but disappeared, laughter's turned to cynicism, the chidlike has given way to the childish. It's all happened in my lifetime and I can't bear it.'

Well, Misty, as the poet said, humankind cannot bear very much reality. As Nick threw himself into his work and play, I retreated into myself, kept my own counsel and, for much of the time when I wasn't on duty, kept to my own room. I wrote a bit and read a lot. I read a book called *Homo Ludens* by Johan Huizinga, a strange study of the place of play in culture. Nick had bought it for me in New York. I thought a good deal about Nick's dream and went back to Jung and *Archetypes and the Collective Unconscious*: 'A more or less superficial layer of the unconscious is undoubtedly personal. I call it the personal unconscious. But this personal unconscious rests upon a deeper layer, which does not derive from personal experience and is not a personal acquisition but is inborn. The deeper layer I call the collective unconscious . . . it has contents and modes of behavior that are more or less the same everywhere and in all individuals.' I pondered long and hard upon the myth of Santa Claus and drew a thick red circle around a paragraph in a book by an analyst called Robert Johnson, a Jungian I had once met with Prof Atkins in San Diego: 'A myth is the collective dream of an entire people at a certain point in their history. It is as though the entire population dreamed together, and that dream, the myth, burst forth through its poetry, songs, and stories. But a myth not only lives in literature and imagination, it immediately finds its way into the behavior and attitudes of the culture – into the practical daily lives of the people.'

At twelve noon on the last Sunday of the semester the faculty was bidden to Dr Thomas Browne's study. As I arrived and was about to knock on the door, I heard the headmaster shout out, 'For Christ's sake, man, pull yourself together.' As a rule when they got drunk, it was Mr Rogers who turned caustic while the Head simply mellowed, then began to stumble and eventually fell. The noise within the room now wasn't of a man falling, but of glasses shattering, as though an angry arm had suddenly swept a tray of them off the buffet. 'You're useless! You've never been anything else! You're shit, pathetic, self-serving shit – a failure, a godforsaken failure. I have loathed you for as long as I've known you and I've known you all my miserable life. Shit, shit, shit.'

The clock began to strike twelve. Theo Quincy appeared behind me and, without pausing or knocking, simply turned the handle and pushed open the door. In the center of Dr Browne's study, surrounded by a wreck of abandoned papers and shattered glass, was the figure of Santa Claus, red-suited, red-faced, arms outstretched, wine bottle in one hand, corkscrew held triumphantly aloft in the other.

'Thank Christ, I've found it!' It was Dr Browne, none too convincingly disguised, none too sober, breathing heavily, but evidently recovering fast from his burst of fury and frustration. 'Merry Christmas, Miss Macdonald. Merry Christmas, Theo. God, how I loathe myself when I put something down and can't remember where or when.'

'It's much worse when you put *someone* down and can't remember who or why!' Theo giggled, and took the bottle and the opener from the Head and set to work.

'Thank you, my boy. It doesn't do for Santa to be butler at his own holiday drinks party.' He maneuvered himself away from the debris and beamed at Theo. 'You shall be Black Peter to my St Nicholas.' The headmaster turned to me and confided, 'Peter's his real name anyway, you know.'

'Why don't you use your real name?'

The cork was out of the bottle. Theo stopped humming 'White Christmas'. 'Because I'm on the run,' he smirked. 'Remember?'

God, these people were infuriating. 'Why does nobody use their own name, for Christ's sake?'

'Not so fast, little Miss Mac. I'll have you know I was baptised Thomas Jefferson Browne. I am who I am!'

Theo switched from *Holiday Inn* to *La Cage aux Folles* and swiveled wild eyes in my direction. I ignored the signal. 'Where does the Doctor bit come from, then?'

'From God. It's divine inspiration.'

'It isn't yours. It isn't honest.'

'Fuck off.'

'I will.'

'Forgive me.' He closed his eyes and shook his head. 'Forgive me, Miss Mac. That's the Grand Marnier talking. I should never drink brandy at breakfast. It brings out the beast in me. I know it excites Miss Haversham, and I so wanted to pleasure her this cool Yuletide, but I should have resisted.'

Miss Haversham was standing at the door. She was framed by it. She was posing there. She was wearing what looked like a wedding dress.

Theo struck up 'Here Comes the Bride' and brandished his bottle in admiration.

'Yes, it is a wedding dress. I've come as Miss Havisham. What do you think? Can I risk it? I want to wear it to Mr Saint's Dickensian evening on Tuesday. I've hired the outfit for the week so I thought I'd try it out on my colleagues first. Verdict?'

'You look ravishing, my dear,' said Dr Browne with emotion.

Theo trilled, 'I see Mr Rogers has come as Uriah Heep.'

'Uriah Heep,' repeated Mr Rogers sourly. He was dressed, of course, exactly as he was always dressed.

'*Ma petite sottise*,' squealed Theo, pouring the last of the red Burgundy into a pair of silver tumblers and handing them to the newcomers. 'Merry Christmas.'

'What's your real name, Miss H?' I was relieved at the way I said it. There was curiosity, not hostility, in the tone.

Miss Haversham was sipping her wine with elaborately pursed lips. 'I've forgotten,' she simpered. 'If I ever knew.'

'If I ever knew,' echoed Mr Rogers, raising his tumbler in the bride's direction.

Miss H was ready to be playful. 'I could tell you Mr Rogers' earlier name,' she said, 'but I won't. I chose his present name for him myself. Will Rogers. It is so inappropriate it appeals to the hidden Dali in my nature.'

'Hello, Dali! This is Salvador, Dali!' Theo uncorked the second bottle and moved effortlessly into his Louis Armstrong impression.

I'd had enough, Misty. 'You're all mad!'

'Bad.'

'And dangerous to know!'

'I can't stand it any longer. I can't take any more of your lies and your fantasies . . .'

'We're nothing but a pack of cards.' Dr Browne was teasing now.

'No, this isn't wonderland. This isn't make-believe. This is hell. This is evil, this is ugly. I can't stand the dishonesty, the never-ending pretenses . . .'

'My dear, our greatest pretenses are built up not to hide the evil and the ugly in us, but our emptiness. "The hardest thing to hide is something that is not there."' The headmaster turned towards Miss Haversham. 'Do you think Eric Hoffer ever stayed at the Chelsea?'

'That's all part of it, isn't it?' I said. 'You all belong to some secret society, don't you? That's why you go to the Chelsea. A sordid secret society set in a seedy hotel. It stinks.'

'It stinks,' sneered Mr Rogers. 'She's sharp, isn't she?'

'It's hardly a secret society,' said Miss Haversham quite kindly. 'It's a dining club. A literary circle, really. The poor man's Algonquin Round Table. It's called the Chelsea Set. Anyone can join.'

'If they've got the imagination.'

'And the style.'

Dr Browne was holding out his tumbler for more. Looking at me with half a smile, he said to Rogers, 'Who could she be?'

'Who could she be?' He didn't pause. 'Lolita.'

'Don't be disgusting.' Miss Haversham was not amused. 'Lolita never stayed at the Chelsea.'

'Nabokov did,' said Dr Browne, 'and we can assume he brought Lolita with him, at least in his imagination. You see, Miss Mac, that's how we play the game. We meet up for dinners at the Chelsea, just three or four times a year, and we each have to spend the evening being somebody who lived there or stayed there or at least had a drink in that god-awful bar. It's only a game.'

'Miss H is usually Sarah Bernhardt and Mr Rogers, *bien*

sûr, is a natural as Andy Warhol.' Theo was replenishing the wine. 'Very boldly, Miss H essayed Mark Twain this last time. It almost came off. Mr Rogers was O. Henry. I don't believe it really worked.'

'Really worked.'

'O. Henry would drink a quart of whiskey a day, you know.' Dr Browne spoke with reverence. 'He was falsely charged with embezzlement and went down for five years. His real name was Porter. He borrowed his new name from one of the penitentiary guards.'

'The headmaster was William Burroughs this time, and read us a wonderful passage from *Dead Fingers Talk*.' Miss Haversham looked lovingly at Dr Browne.

'I was Tennessee Williams – again!' said Theo cheerfully. 'I was exceptional, as usual, but, as usual, it was Father Sebastian who stole the show. He was Dylan Thomas. He was magical. He recited the whole of *A Child's Christmas in Wales* from memory.'

'Is Nicodemus Barclay a member?' I asked.

'Good God, no!' Dr Browne held out his tumbler once more. 'It's a club for intellectuals, bohemians, scholars and gentlefolk, not shyster billionaires. Our interest in Mr Barclay is entirely financial.' Theo was ready with the third bottle. The headmaster was mellowing again. 'People go on murder weekends, people go on dirty weekends. People fly to Disneyland and Havana and God knows where. We just pootle off to a down-at-heel hotel and spend a night or two conjuring up its ghosts, pretending our lives are a touch more remarkable than they really are, dipping ourselves briefly into the cup of genius that appears to have passed us by.'

'We don't do no one no harm, missy.'

'But you have done, Theo, haven't you?'

'I don't think so.' Miss Haversham stepped towards me.

'*Crime passionel*,' said Theo.

Miss Haversham was close by me now. I looked at her and said, 'That painting in the faculty room. That doesn't belong to you, Miss H. It isn't yours.'

'It isn't anybody's.'

'Yes, it is.'

'Property is theft.'

'For God's sake.' I was ready to scream, Misty. I suppose I was drunk too. 'I've worked it out. It wasn't difficult.'

'It was *very* difficult.' Miss H was playing it cool: the bride as ice maiden. 'Removing a Burne-Jones from a private collection without anyone noticing was very difficult indeed. My finest hour.'

'Your final throw,' I said. 'That's why you disappeared here, isn't it? There was nowhere else to hide. When it was just clocks and watches, it was so much easier, so much less conspicuous.'

'You appear to be under a misapprehension, Miss Macdonald. We never stole anything. All we did was give expert advice. We provided attributions – as required. William specialized in clocks. I specialized in nineteenth-century painting. Sometimes we got it wrong. We're only human.'

'You told Mrs Whitney Miller that her Burne-Jones wasn't a Burne-Jones after all.'

'And who's to say whether I was right or wrong? The Mona Lisa now on show in the Louvre in Paris isn't by the hand of Leonardo. True or false? The original went missing in 1911 and wasn't seen for fifteen months. Are you certain who painted the picture that's hanging in its place today? If it looks like the real thing, who's to say it isn't the real thing? Our old friend Elmyr de Hory fooled the market for years with his Picassos and his Matisses and his Modiglianis. No one got hurt. It didn't matter. It doesn't matter.'

'It does matter. It does!' Was I shouting now? I'm ashamed to say, Misty, I think I might have been. 'There's right and there's wrong, and saying something is one thing when you know it to be another is wrong, plain wrong.'

'Plain wrong. That's an interesting expression.' Mr Rogers narrowed his eyes and the thin lines around them darkened, as though tiny spiders were trying to crawl out of his eye sockets. 'No, Miss Madconald, you simply don't understand.' He ran his Burgundy tongue deliberately along his upper lip. 'A clock is a clock is a clock. If it tells the time, it's true. Who cares if it's a Bodel or a Gubelin? Only the auctioneer and the vendor and the purchaser, and they're all as greedy and venal as each other. I merely told them what they wanted to hear.'

'That's what lies are. Don't you see? Telling people what they want to hear is wrong if what they want to hear isn't true.'

'So,' said Dr Browne conclusively, as if bringing the board meeting to a satisfactory close, 'That's why you're leaving us. Because you cannot tell a lie. George Washington would have been proud of you.'

'Are you going, Kirsty?'

'Yes, Theo. Miss Macdonald has all the virtues, including that of resignation. I received her sad little note last night.'

'Have you told Mr Saint that you're going?' Miss Haversham asked the question.

'No, I haven't.' I hesitated. 'Not yet.' I looked about the room. I was quite drunk by now. 'Where is he?'

'I believe he's gone to New York for the day,' said Dr Browne with a thin smile. 'I imagine he's visiting your sick sister.'

Chapter Fifteen

The art of correspondence may be in terminal decline, but for cowards and lovers letters still have their uses. The note I had left on Dr Browne's desk the night before had been both cowardly and brief to the point of discourtesy. I didn't know quite what to say or how best to say it, so I had simply tendered my resignation in five trite sentences. I provided neither a proper explanation ('I just don't feel it's working out') nor any kind of justification for my failure to honor my contractual obligation by offering at least a semester's notice ('I am afraid I will be unable to return in January'). Archly, gracelessly, I just about managed to say thank you and sorry ('Thank you for the opportunity you have given me. I am sorry for any inconvenience my departure will cause'), but the paragraph as a whole did me little credit either as a correspondent or as a colleague.

The letter I wrote to Nick that Sunday night was a great deal longer, perhaps less cowardly, certainly more confused. I am embarrassed to recall it now, Misty, because my opening line was so absurdly melodramatic. 'Nick, I am writing to say goodbye.' Ye gods! 'I have decided to leave Magnolia Hall because I can't see the point of staying. Probably I shouldn't have come in the first place. I'm glad I came, of course, because meeting you has been the most EXTRAORDINARY experience of my life. Also the most frustrating! You are amazing, we all know that! – handsome, kind, funny, cute – why can I write these things when I can never say them? You're so perfect you're unreal. That's the problem. I seem to have let myself fall in love with someone who isn't there! I keep asking myself if I am really in love with you? If being in love with someone is thinking about them morning, noon and night, wanting to be with them, wanting to know them, to understand them, to be inside them, heart and mind and soul, then I'm certainly in love with you, Nick. Does that embarrass you? Probably! If so, I apologize. I've been in love before and I know being in love and loving are different – Prof Atkins used to say that "being in love" is the journey and "loving" the destination – and I suppose that's what's wrong – at least from my point of view. We're not going anywhere. Do you love me? Who knows? I doubt if you know yourself. I know you like me, I know it feels good when we're together, you sometimes even seem to fancy me (sorry!) but I also know you're holding back. It's more than a fear of seduction. There's something that you can't, won't, give. Maybe you're frightened of being hurt. Maybe you're frightened of hurting. Maybe it really is because you don't know who you are. Whatever it is, Nick, we've hit the glass ceiling. It's going nowhere, and before I get hurt I'm getting out. Do you remember Theo telling us that the average length of an affair is three months? Well, we've had our twelve weeks and it's been FANTASTIC. I love you, Nick. You are the sun and the moon and the stars – you may even be Santa Claus for all I know! (No, Nick, you can't be Santa Claus – any more than I can be Cinderella. Santa Claus is a mythical character. You've got to accept that. How you learn to accept it, I'm not sure. I thought I could help you, but I can't. Someone like Dr Hofmann could. Don't get mad at me! I know you're not a paranoid schizophrenic, but believing you're Santa or Jesus or Sherlock Holmes is definitely UNUSUAL and letting the feeling rule your life is dangerous, and I think you do need help. Okay, now I've said it you'll never want to speak to me again. Hey, a week from now you'll never have to speak to me again! I'll have disappeared and you'll be free! I don't know what I'm saying, Nick. I'm like those stupid women who fall in love with priests. I'm wanting to dream the impossible dream. And you ARE dreaming the impossible dream! This is crazy.')

It was a crazy letter, Misty, from a crazy woman to a crazy man at a crazy time in both their crazy lives. It took hours to write and ran to many pages. Some of it made sense, much of it didn't. Halfway through writing it I began to cry. Like blobs of glycerine, hot, heavy tears poured down my cheeks onto the paper. It was weariness as well as love and hurt and self-indulgence. I wrote through the tears and beyond the tears and by the time I had finished – 'I LOVE YOU, I LOVE YOU, I LOVE YOU, NICK SAINT, WHOEVER YOU ARE' – it was nearly midnight and I don't think I knew what I really felt anymore. I couldn't fold the pages, there were too many of them, so I took them as they were, wrapped in a bit of ribbon, and, like a dad creeping into his kids' room with the Christmas stocking, I stepped as softly as I could across the tiny landing to Nick's door. I stood in a sort of daze, wondering, I suppose, if I should risk leaving the letter on the floor or if I should try to wedge it under the door, when I watched the handle turn and looked up and there he was. He smiled a gentle smile. He looked different. At the time I couldn't work out why. Later I realized. He looked tired, exhausted, less god-like, more human.

'I thought I heard someone,' he said. 'Are you okay?'

'I'm fine. I—'

'I went to New York today.'

'Yes,' I said. 'I heard.'

'I'm sorry I didn't tell you. I couldn't.'

'I understand.'

'There were things I had to do.'

'I know.'

'I had to get it sorted.'

'And did you?'

'No, Kirsty. No, I didn't. And now I'm running out of time.'

'I'm sorry.'

'At least I saw them.'

'Who did you see?'

'Both of them.'

'Nicodemus Barclay?'

'Yes. And Dr Hofmann.'

You guessed. I did not give him my letter. I simply said goodnight and went to bed and slept one of those deep, vacant, guiltless sleeps that come when you least expect them and need them most. In the morning the winter sun shone and Nick Saint looked his golden self again. For the next three days he played Adonis to the manner born. He was gorgeous. There was laughter and energy and warmth when he was there. However Augustus St George defined star quality, Nick had it. The stage was brighter when he was on it. His part of the screen was where your eye fell.

You will be relieved to learn, Misty, that though I decided to play a part myself that week it was more Admiring Kid Sister than Aphrodite. ('To an extent happiness is a habit, like good posture, so you will benefit from a routine that includes walking tall with a smile on your face. You can become the part you play, so choose the part with care' *Act It/Be It – Role-playing Strategies to get you through the Day*, A. A. Atkins, 1978.) The highlight of the pre-Christmas festivities at Magnolia Hall was the Dickensian evening on Tuesday night. It wasn't so much a party as a concert, with the faculty and boys all in costume doing turns, while the parents, guardians and chauffeurs looked on, bemused strangers, impatient for the entertainment to be over so they could collect their charges and scram. Adonis (as David Copperfield), with Miss H (as Miss Havisham) on his arm, stole the show with ease. Dr Browne was a credible Fagin (a good wig works wonders) and, surrounded by the younger boys, performed a number from the musical *Oliver!* with surprising style. Less convincingly, Mr Rogers (an incredible Mr Pickwick – Miss H's idea!) led the carol-singing. As Bill Sykes and Nancy, Theo and I ran riot – or as riot as you run on two glasses of mulled wine at the end-of-year gathering at a boys' private school in South Carolina. The evening ended touchingly with Nick holding Żanu high above his shoulders and the little Saudi Arabian princeling shouting out, 'God bless us every one!'

Wednesday was the day for fond farewells – fond yet formal. None of my colleagues had questioned my decision to move on. Each had expressed perfunctory regret, even Mr Rogers, but that wasn't so surprising. We were simply fellow travelers, after all, voyagers thrown together for the duration of the cruise. We'd been quite intimate to be sure, there were nights when we'd all let our hair down together, told tall tales, let cats out of bags, let indiscretions fly, family secrets even, but that was then and this was now. On vacation different rules apply. As we said goodbye, we promised to keep in touch, knowing we didn't mean it.

Nick had offered to drive me up to Dulles for my flight to LA. He carried my cases to the car and, like an old-fashioned Southern guy, held the door open for me as I got in. At the window of his study, Dr Browne held back the drapes and, as promised, raised an American Beauty in a dutiful farewell toast.

As the old Mercedes scrunched the gravel and Magnolia Hall evaporated behind us, Nick, playing the best of buddies, laughed his carefree laugh and asked, 'Do you know what that rascal has been up to?'

'Dr Browne?'

'Yes, Dr Browne, the old rogue. You'll never believe it, you'll never guess. He's been trying to sell the school – to Nicodemus Barclay!'

'What would he want a school for?'

'He doesn't. It's the last thing he wants. It was Dr Browne's idea entirely. An idea designed to solve all our revered headmaster's financial difficulties at a stroke. Keep the place going as a school, but at the same time sell it to 7 Cs and throw it open to the public as a unique visitor attraction, an eccentric period piece.'

'*Tom Brown's Schooldays* come to life.'

'Exactly. Magnolia Hall as a kind of living museum and academic theme park – a sort of educational Williamsburg – "an eighteenth-century setting for nineteenth-century values at twentieth-century prices"!'

'Wow!'

'That's what Barclay thought. Dr Browne just wrote to

him out of the blue and the great entrepreneur agreed to meet him and Rogers because the idea seemed so outrageous that he was intrigued. I don't think Mr Barclay was seriously tempted for a moment, but he said he thought it could work. As you'll recall, he's a great believer in the power of the well-marketed brand name.'

'Is that why you went to see him?'

'No.' Nick hesitated. 'I went because he asked.'

'How did he know where to get hold of you?'

'He didn't.'

I wasn't going to probe any more. Why should I? I let the air hang heavy with one of those dumb silences where you count the seconds in your head and swear to yourself you'll never speak again unless he does first. Before I got to fifteen, he did.

'Do you remember the books he gave us the Sunday we went to see him? He wrote a message in mine.'

'Yes?'

'"Happy Birthday. Call sometime." So I called and I went. And as I arrived, who should be leaving? Yup. Our old friend, Dr David Hofmann.'

'What did he want to talk about?'

'Barclay? Barclay wanted to talk about you.' I didn't say anything. I looked straight ahead. We were on the turnpike now. 'He wanted to know everything I knew about you. He wanted to know where we'd met and when and how. He wanted to know if I was in love with you.' You'd have been proud of me, Misty. I held the silence. I started counting. 'And he offered me a job.'

I did not say, 'Nick Saint, do you love me?' I did not say, 'What did you tell Nico Barclay about me and why?' I simply stopped counting and asked, 'What kind of job?'

'He said he'd put me in charge of the Santa Claus project.'

'Christ almighty, Nick! Can't you think of anything else?' I didn't know whether to laugh or scream or cry.

'No, no, don't get me wrong. He wasn't pandering to my fantasy. This was for real. He's using computer games and videos to carry subliminal messages that stimulate the brain to release endorphins. He plans to use the technique to promote his personal vision of Santa Claus.'

'Is he mad?'

'Possibly. He told me the word "endorphin" is a contraction of "endogenous morphine". He talked a lot about morphine. He kept saying, "More morphine, more feelgood." He said it again and again. It was horrible.'

'Doesn't the brain produce endorphins quite naturally?'

'Sure, that's the point. They come naturally, they can relieve pain, they can ease anxiety, they can produce a high – and Mr Barclay has found you can get hooked on them. "It's all just a matter of harnessing nature. Let the peptides do the talking. It's merely morphine for the masses – and it's all home grown."'

'It's sick.'

'It's easy. You buy the computer game, you play it. On the soundtrack there's a mesmerising beat and, beneath the beat, inaudible to the conscious ear, subliminal hypnotic messages, hundreds of them. The messages trigger the endorphins.'

'What do they say?'

'"I feel good", "I am good", "I am innocent", "I am never guilty", "I can do what I want", "I can have what I want", "I can have it when I want it", "I want it", "I want it now." That's the kind of thing they say this year.

Next year they'll be saying much the same, only more so, and with the added attraction of subliminal images of the 7 Cs version of Santa Claus being transmitted at the climactic moments.'

'What's the point?'

'Power. Money. The kids become entranced, literally. They seem hooked on the game, but in fact it's the high they're hooked on. More morphine, more feelgood. They're turned on and they can't let go. They play one game, then they need another. And another. And only 7 Cs make them. It's like a drug, but according to Nicodemus Barclay it's all quite legal. "Games so good, they're addictive!" He's a bad man, Kirsty, even if he is my father.'

'Is he your father?'

'I think so. I'm not sure.'

Snow was falling, snow on snow. As the tiny flakes landed gently on the windscreen, filigree petals past our devisal ('My head is full of stuff – so much stuff – and I don't know where half of it comes from'), we fell silent inside the car, but it was an easy silence now, soft, comforting almost, like the snow. We were ninety miles from the Dulles turnoff. That's what the roadsign said, so why was Nick, quite suddenly, moving off the highway here, now? I looked at him. He was smiling. A private joke.

'Don't worry. You'll catch your flight.'

Within a quarter of an hour we seemed to have journeyed to the far side of the moon, from bright lights to blackout, from somewhere to nowhere. We came off the highway onto one ancillary road, onto another, onto a third, then, quite quickly, off again to a small country road, then sharp left, onto an unmarked lane, untrammeled, a deserted single track.

Nick stopped the car. 'This is it. Come on.'

The snow had stopped falling. The air was still and cold and clear. I looked up at the moon and watched it disappear at once behind a cloud.

'This way.'

Nick had a flashlight in one hand. He took me in the other and led me off the track towards the trees.

'It's through the wood.'

We walked for five minutes, no more, watching our breath steam out ahead of us, listening to the snap and scrunch of our footfalls as we waded through branch and bracken, brittle and rimed. At last we reached a clearing in the wood. It was vast, a football field covered in frosted sugar, with, right at its center, cut out against the sky like a distorted Disney castle, a sprawling mansion, magnificent but definitely misshapen, brick and wood and stucco, all heaped together in a bizarre mishmash of styles – Federal, Gothic, Queen Anne. The house was broad and wide and high – three stories high at least – with pointed gables, tall brick chimneys, turrets, towers and what looked like large encircling verandas on each floor. Right at the front, up on the first level, standing out on the balcony, silhouetted against a lighted window, was the figure of a man, tall and slight, taking the night air.

Nick closed the flashlight against his chest and whispered, 'Don't say a word.'

Slowly, oh-so-slowly, we crept around the perimeter of the clearing, edging our way towards the house, hugging the frosted fringe of the wood until, abruptly, the trees gave way to a high brick wall. It was an old, worn, rough, red-brick wall, the kind that might have guarded Mr MacGregor's vegetable patch. We stayed in the safety of its shadow as we inched our way onwards.

We were parallel with the front of the house, about fifty yards from the wide front steps leading to the darkened veranda, when the wall transformed itself into an elegant sandstone archway that led immediately to a cobbled stable yard. Suddenly, silently, the whole yard was bathed in silver light. The cloud had lifted from the moon and around the square of ice-covered cobblestones we saw, with complete clarity, a curious assortment of wooden barns and brick outbuildings.

Sharply, Nick pulled me inside the nearest door. At once the air was heavy with the comforting stench of the stable. The warmth, the smell, the rustle of the animals, it felt good. In the half-light we could see the stalls. One of the beasts shook itself and clattered its hooves impatiently on the cold stone floor. Nick shone his flashlight towards the animal and lit up the giant eyes, the heavy head, the lugubrious jaw of a huge and handsome reindeer. Nick flashed his light around the stable. There was stall after stall, five, six, seven or more, and reindeer tethered in each. Nick played the light along the floor, over the walls, across the high vaulted ceiling. At the far end of the stable, about ten feet off the ground, was a kind of half-floor, like a wide ledge, jutting out into the stable, and on it, gleaming in the broad beam of the flashlight, displayed like a model car in a plastic case, was a beautiful wooden sleigh, polished and painted, bright like new. Nick's light caught the narrow ladder that reached up from the stable to the half-floor. He ran to it and climbed it and almost threw himself upon the sleigh. He ran his hands over the wood, caressing it; he stroked the harness; gently he lifted the reins and, softly, the bells began to jingle-jangle. 'Kirsty,' he whispered, 'look!' On the seat of the sleigh, neatly folded, were a pair of tiny white cotton gloves carefully placed on top of a small fur-trimmed red cape. He turned, triumphant, and held out his trophies. 'Kirsty!' he called, much louder this time. 'Kirsty, look!'

I couldn't answer, Misty. An ice-cold black hand had covered my mouth and Rocky was pulling me, dragging me, hard, across the stable yard towards the house.

'Kirsty! Kirsty!' I heard Nick call again. I heard him jump from the ledge down into the stable, I heard the stable door yanked open, I heard his steps, clear and fast, as he came running after me.

Rocky had pulled me as far as the foot of the wide white steps leading up to the veranda when Nick fell onto him. My hero didn't say a word. He simply took Rocky by the shoulders, pulled him back, turned him round and hit him with terrifying force so that he simply crumpled and fell in a heap into the snow at the foot of the steps.

'Are you playing Santa Claus or Superman today?' asked Nicodemus Barclay from the balcony. 'I don't believe James Bond went around beating up middle-aged black guys in the dark.'

Nick stepped back and gazed up at the elegant figure of the reclusive billionaire. 'I'm not playing anybody. I just want to play myself.'

'Whoever that may be.'

'Exactly. Can you tell me who I am?'

Slowly Barclay blew a thin flume of cigar smoke out into the night air. He was toying with the moment. 'Yes, Nick, I think so. I think old Nico Barclay can help you there.'

'Are you my father?'

He waited. He leant against the balustrade and then he said it, clearly, without equivocation. 'Yes. Yes, Nick, I'm your dad. I shouldn't have been, of course. Perhaps you guessed?' He held the pause. 'Sebastian should have been your father. He was born to be your father. That was to be his destiny. But I got there first. Charlotte Richards fell for the wrong guy. It sometimes happens.'

'And how do you know who I am? How do you know I'm not just some crazy mixed-up kid who's after your millions?'

'I knew who you were the moment I set eyes on you, Nick, the moment I saw you wearing her ring. You're a crazy mixed-up kid, that's for sure, but you're my son and you're not certifiable. I know. I checked. Dr Hofmann suspects you may be as sane as he is.'

Nick laughed. 'So who am I?'

'Do you really want to know?'

'I really want to know!'

'You're who you always thought you were. You're Santa Claus, Nick. You always have been. And your mother was Santa Claus before you. And her father was Santa Claus before her. It goes from mother to son across the generations. I thought I could break the spell.'

'Did you kill her?'

'No. Yes. No. She had the morphine. I gave her more. I played my part. We all did. The sixties killed Charlie Richards, the sixties murdered Santa Claus. For a generation the light went out. The routine of Christmas went on, of course, but the spirit of Christmas disappeared. It was always the parents who had filled the stockings, but it was Santa who brought the magic. Suddenly Santa went missing. The parents went on giving the presents, but they didn't seem to mean so much. Santa Claus went AWOL for twenty-nine years and the world paid the price. Hadn't you noticed?'

Nico Barclay dropped his cigar into the snow and leaned

out over the balcony. 'Goodbye, son. I'm going now. Can I ask you something before I leave? Will you forgive me? I'm not a bad man, you know. I may not be a good man like Sebastian, but I'm not evil. Don't think that. Lost, okay. Wrong, yes. But not evil. I don't buy that stuff about Santa being an anagram of Satan, do you?'

'No, Dad.' Nick was smiling through the tears.

'Well done, my boy. You've come to claim your inheritance.' He lifted his arms and spun round and called out to the night, 'Santa's come home! Santa's back! All's right with the world!' In the room behind him, a clock began to strike. 'You won't ever see me again, but you'll think of me, Nick, won't you?' He waved, and smiled, and walked through the French windows back into the house. We never saw him again.

We turned and saw that Rocky had gone, too. Suddenly, behind us, there was the clatter of hooves. Rocky, upright, beaming, was leading the reindeer to the front of the house.

As he held out his hand to help me into the sleigh, Nick smiled and said, 'I said you'd catch your flight.'

The clock in the upstairs room chimed one hundred.

'Can you remember their names, Kirsty?' He picked up the reins and threw back his beautiful head and roared, 'Now Dasher, now Dancer, now Prancer and Vixen! On Comet, on Cupid, on Donner and Blitzen!'

And off we flew, Misty, up, up and away, through the snow, through the clouds, towards the stars, straight on till morning. It was the night before Christmas and we encircled the globe. And as we flew, higher and higher, in every window in every house in every country we saw candles being lit, one by one, all over the world.

When we were flying over Manhattan, over Chelsea,

and we could see the little church of St Nicholas far, far below, my hero put his hand in mind and said, 'If we get through tonight, if we manage to land this thing safely, would you consider marrying me? You see, I know who I am and I know who you are, and, Kirsty Macdonald, I love you.'

'And I love you, Santa Claus.'

And, Misty, your dad and I, we love you too. So much. We just wanted you to know how you got here. It's your turn next. Awesome, huh?